Eyewitness
SOCCER

1930s French hair-oil advertisement

1905 match holder

1900s soccer ball pumps

Jay Jay Okocha of Nigeria

1900s shin pads

1910s shin pads

1930s shin pads

Early 20th-century soccer ball stencils

1966 World Cup soccer ball

1930s painting of a goalkeeper

1998 World Cup soccer ball

Early 20th-
century
porcelain
figure

Early 20th-
century
porcelain
figure

Eyewitness
SOCCER

Written by
HUGH HORNBY

Photographed by
ANDY CRAWFORD

1912 soccer ball

in association with
THE NATIONAL FOOTBALL MUSEUM, UK

19th-century jersey

1925 Australian International shirt

1905 book cover image

1900s plaster figure

DK

LONDON, NEW YORK,
MELBOURNE, MUNICH, AND DELHI

Project editor Louise Pritchard
Art editor Jill Plank
Assistant editor Annabel Blackledge
Assistant art editor Yolanda Belton
Managing art editor Sue Grabham
Senior managing art editor Julia Harris
Production Kate Oliver
Picture research Amanda Russell
DTP Designer Andrew O'Brien and Georgia Bryer

THIS EDITION
Consultants Mark Bushell, David Goldblatt
Editors Kitty Blount, Sarah Philips, Sue Nicholson,
Victoria Heywood-Dunne, Marianne Petrou
Art editors Andrew Nash, David Ball
Managing editors Andrew Macintyre, Camilla Hallinan
Managing art editors Jane Thomas, Martin Wilson
Publishing manager Sunita Gahir
Production editors Siu Yin Ho, Andy Hilliard
Production controllers Jenny Jacoby, Pip Tinsley
DK picture library Rose Horridge, Myriam Megharbi, Emma Shepherd
Picture research Carolyn Clerkin, Will Jones
U.S. editorial Beth Hester, John Searcy
U.S. publishing director Beth Sutinis
U.S. design and D.T.P. Dirk Kaufman, Milos Orlovic
U.S. production Chris Avgherinos, Ivor Parker

This Eyewitness ® Guide has been conceived by
Dorling Kindersley Limited and Editions Gallimard

This edition published in the United States in 2005, 2008
by DK Publishing Inc., 375 Hudson Street, New York, New York 10014

A catalog record for this book is
available from the Library of Congress.

ISBN: 978-07566-3779-8 (Hardcover)
978-0-7566-1092-0 (Library Binding)

Color reproduction by Colourscan, Singapore
Printed and bound by Leo Paper Products Ltd., China

Discover more at
www.dk.com

1908 Newcastle shirt

1900s silver match holder

1930s silver hatpin

1920s silver flint lighter

Early 20th-century snap card

THE REFEREE

Shirts from 1890s catalog

Contents

Hungary badge
Holland badge
Italy badge
Brazil badge

Early 20th-century child's rattle

1930s child's painted rattle

The global game

SOCCER HAS ITS ROOTS IN ancient China, Europe, and the Americas. People kicked a ball to prepare for war, to honor their gods, or just to entertain themselves. For centuries, different versions of ball-kicking games existed. In Europe, they were tests of courage and strength and in China and other Eastern countries, the games were rituals of grace and skill. The rules of the modern game of soccer were not drawn up until 1863, but the qualities that we admire in it—speed, agility, bravery, and spirit—have been present in many cultures for more than 2,000 years.

It's a good old game
Deny it who can

An Ashbourne ball

ASHBOURNE BALL
Ashbourne in Derbyshire, England. is the site of one of several traditional Mardi Gras soccer games. It is characterized by disorder. Two teams, the Upwards and the Downwards, try to move the ball through the opposition's "goal"—a gateway at the other end of town.

HARROW BALL
English private schools, including Harrow and Eton, played a crucial role in developing modern soccer in the early 1800s. Although each school played the game differently, they all produced detailed, written rules. These provided the basis for the first official rules.

The Harrow ball was flattened, top and bottom, to allow it to skim across muddy playing fields.

SOCCER TRAINING
The Chinese were playing a type of soccer by the 3rd century BC. A military book of that period refers to *tsu chu*, or "kicking a ball." The game may once have been part of a soldier's training and was later included in ceremonies on the emperor's birthday.

These symbols were once described by an official of the English Football Association as "To kick with the foot"

足球

Chinese characters meaning "soccer"

A GENTLEMEN'S GAME
The game of calcio was played in Italian cities such as Venice and Florence in the 16th and 17th centuries. On certain festival days, two teams of gentlemen would attempt to force the ball through openings at either end of a city square. Although physical contact was a feature of calcio, the game also had a tactical element. Teams used formations and attempted to create space in which to advance.

Local people came out to watch the games

Handling the ball was part of the game

Players have to
wear an elaborate
costume of silk
and gold brocade

Ball made
from strips
of leather

Men from many different
backgrounds played soccer

STREET GAMES
This early 19th-century cartoon is subtitled "Dustmen, coalmen,
gentlemen, and city clerks at murderous if democratic play". It shows the
violent "every man for himself" spirit common to street games in Britain
at that time. The damage done to property, particularly windows, and the
disruption to the lives of other citizens caused many town councils to ban
soccer—without much success.

ANCIENT RITUAL
The Japanese game of kemari probably developed in the 7th
century from an ancient Chinese soccer game, after contact was
made between the two countries. In contrast to the chaotic
early soccer brawls of Europe, it involved many rituals
and was played as part of a ceremony. The game
is still played today and involves keeping the ball
in the air inside a small court.

Kemari is a game
of balance and skill

SOCCER WRITING
Soccer has been a popular literary
subject for as long as the game has
been played. The first-known book
devoted to soccer is *Discourse on calcio*
by Giovanni da Bardi, published in 1580
in Florence, Italy. Soccer has inspired
poetry, too. "A Match
at Soccer" by
Matthew Concanen
was published in an
anthology in the 18th
century. The popularity
of soccer increased
rapidly in the early
20th century. *The School
Across the Road* by
Desmond Coke
is one of many
children's books
published at around
that time.

16th-century
discourse on
soccer

18th-century
anthology

Image from a
9th-century
watercolor
on silk

The children's
book *The School
Across the Road*

Color plates appear
throughout the book

History of soccer

THE GAME THAT HAS CAPTURED the imaginations of people all over the world was developed in England and Scotland in the 19th century. The former pupils of English private schools produced the first common set of rules for football, or soccer, and formed the Football Association (FA) in 1863. Things moved forward quickly. British administrators, merchants, and engineers took the game overseas and people from other countries began to play soccer. The first international games were followed by professional leagues and big competitions.

Kinnaird once did a headstand after winning a Cup final

CELEBRITY PLAYER
The first players were amateurs. C. B. Fry, who played for the Corinthians in the late 1890s, was one of the first soccer celebrities. He was also a member of the England cricket team and held the world long-jump record.

Arnold Kirke Smith's cap

EXHIBITIONISM
Throughout the early years of the 20th century, British teams toured the world, introducing soccer to other countries by playing exhibition games. This shield was presented to the Islington Corinthians in Japan, in 1937.

The English Three Lions motif was first used in 1872

Arnold Kirke Smith's England shirt

The shirt is made of closely woven wool

THE FIRST INTERNATIONAL
In November 1872, Scotland played England on a cricket field in Glasgow in the first-ever international match. About 2, 000 spectators watched a 0–0 draw. This shirt and cap were worn by Arnold Kirke Smith from Oxford University, who was a member of the English team.

MODERN RULES
Lord Kinnaird was President of the Football Association from 1890–1923, and was one of the amateurs who shaped the rules and structure of the modern game. Previously, he had played in nine of the first l2 FA Cup finals, winning five.

TALENTED TEAMS
The English Football League began in 1888. Its 12-team fixture program was inspired by US baseball. This 1893 painting by Thomas Hemy shows two successful clubs of the 1890s: Aston Villa, which won the league five times and Sunderland, "the team of all talents," which won three times.

In reality, women's uniforms were far less figure-hugging

A ball of exaggerated size

THE UNRULY GAME
The first French soccer league, set up in 1894, was dominated by teams of Scottish emigrants, such as the White Rovers and Standard AC. French satirists were quick to refer to the game's reputation for unruliness. This 1900s French magazine, *Le Monde Comique*, reflects this attitude toward the game.

Bystanders often got caught up in the boisterous action

Cover illustration entitled "*Les Plaisirs du Dimanche*" ("Sunday" Pleasures")

LADIES FIRST
Women's soccer started at the end of the 19th century. Teams such as the British Ladies' Club attracted large crowds. During the World War I, men's and women's teams played against each other for charity. The first women's World Cup was held in China in 1991 and was won by the USA.

FIFA badge

FORMING FIFA
By 1904, several countries, including France, Belgium, Denmark, the Netherlands, Spain, Sweden, and Switzerland had their own administrators. They formed the world governing body, FIFA (Fédération Internationale de Soccer Associations). By 1939, more than 50 countries had joined.

This 1900s plaster figure is wearing shin pads that were typical of that time

Ugandan batik

OUT OF AFRICA
Soccer spread through Africa from both ends of the continent. South Africa, with its European populations, was an obvious foothold and sent a touring party to South America in 1906. In 1923, Egypt, in North Africa, was the first African team to join FIFA.

Each stamp shows a different US player

US stamps produced for the 1994 World Cup

SOCCER
Youth soccer is the most widely played sport in the US, for both boys and girls. The 1994 World Cup provided a big boost for Major League Soccer, which is bringing top-level professional games to a new audience. The US reached the semifinals of the very first World Cup in 1930.

Laws of the game

THE RULES OF A GAME should be brief and easy to understand. It is certain that soccer's success has been partly due to the simplicity of its Laws. Rules governing equipment, the field, foul play, and restarts have all survived the passage of time. Soccer has always been a free-flowing game. Stoppages can be avoided if the referee uses the advantage rule—allowing play to continue after a foul, provided that the right team still has the ball. The offside rule has always been a source of controversy in the game. The assistant referees must make split-second decisions about whether an attacker has strayed beyond the second-to-last defender at the moment the ball is played forward by one of his or her teammates. A player cannot be offside from a throw-in.

STAND BACK
This throw-in is illegal. The ball is held correctly in both hands but the feet, though they are both on the ground as they should be, are over the line.

There have been goal posts since the early days of soccer but, until the crossbar was introduced in 1875, tape was stretched between them 8 ft (2.5 m) from the ground

The penalty spot is 12 yd (11 m) from the goal line

Goal kicks must be taken from within the 6-yd (5.5-m) box

Players must not cross the half-way line until the ball is kicked off

PENALTY
Penalties were introduced in 1891 as a punishment for foul play, such as tripping, pushing, or handball within 12 yd (11 m) of the goal. A player shoots at goal from the penalty spot with only the goal-keeper to beat. If the ball rebounds from the post or bar the penalty taker cannot play it again before someone else has touched it.

FREE KICK
There are two types of free kick—direct and indirect. In an indirect free kick, awarded after an infringement of a Law, the ball must be touched by two players before a goal is scored. Direct free kicks are given after fouls and the taker may score immediately. Opposing players must be at least 10 yd (9 m) away from the ball at a free kick.

CORNER
A corner kick is taken when the defending team puts the ball out of play behind its own goal-line. Corner kicks provide useful goal-scoring opportunities. The ball must be placed within the quadrant—a quarter circle with a radius of 1 yd (1 m) in the corner of the field. A goal can be scored directly from a corner kick.

FAKING FOULS
The amateur players of the 19th century believed that all fouls were accidental and would have been horrified by the "professional foul," an offense deliberately committed to prevent an attack from developing. Unfortunately, the game today is full of deliberate fouls. Some players also fake being fouled to get their team a free kick.

When a penalty is taken, only the taker is allowed inside the "D"

CHARGE!
The 1958 English FA Cup final between Manchester United and Bolton Wanderers is remembered for the disputed goal scored by Bolton's center-forward, Nat Lofthouse. He charged the United goalkeeper, Harry Gregg, over the line as he caught the ball—a challenge that all referees today would consider a foul.

Players from the defending team must stay out of the 10-yd (9-m) circle before the kickoff

Players cannot be offside in their own half of the field

The 6-yd (5.5-m) box was semicircular until 1902. The penalty box was introduced in the same year

A goalkeeper is restricted to four steps when kicking a ball out of the hands

Assistant referees patrol opposite sides of the field and cover one half each, their main responsibilities being to signal throw-ins and flag for offside

PERMANENT MARKERS
In the mid-19th century, before it was stipulated that permanent lines should be marked on the field, flags were used as a guide to whether the ball was out of play. Today, a corner flag has to be at least 5 ft (1.5 m) high so players do not risk being impaled.

LAW AND ORDER
There are 17 main soccer Laws. The field of play must be rectangular and, for a full-size field, from 110 to 120 yd (100.5 to 110 m) long and from 70 to 80 yd (64 to 73 m) wide. There should be 11 players per side. Substitution rules have changed over the years and teams may now substitute any three from five players, including the goalie, during stoppages in the match. The duration of play is 90 minutes, in two halves of 45 minutes each.

Goal nets, patented by Brodies of Liverpool, England, in 1891, were first officially used in 1892 and were welcomed as a means of settling disputes over whether a ball had actually entered the goal

The referee

EARLY AMATEUR players put a high value on fair play but saw the need for officials on the soccer field. To begin with, each team provided an umpire from its own club, who did not interfere much with the passage of play. At this stage, players had to raise an arm and appeal for a decision if they felt that they had been fouled, otherwise play continued. The rise of professional soccer in the 1880s made it harder for umpires to be neutral. A referee was introduced to settle disputes. In 1891, the referee was moved onto the field of play and the umpires became linesmen, a system that has continued ever since. Linesmen and women are now called assistant referees.

Early 20th-century playing card caricature of a referee

YOUR NUMBER'S UP
One duty of the assistant referees is to control the entrance of substitutes to the field, checking their studs and indicating with number cards which player is to be replaced. At top levels of the game, a fourth official uses an illuminated board to indicate substitutes and inform everyone how much injury time will be played at the end of each half.

CLASSIC BLACK
This is the classic referee's uniform, all-black with white cuffs and collar. Dating from the 1970s, this uniform is similar to all those worn after the phasing out of the blazer in the 1940s to the introduction of other colors in the 1990s. The bulky jackets of the early 1900s were replaced by a less constricting shirt to encourage the officials to keep up with play on the field.

White trim sets off the all-black uniform

Notebook to record bookings, goals, sendings off, and substitutions

The yellow card is shown for bookable offenses

Serious foul play results in a red card and a sending off

1940s Acme whistle

Both sides of a FIFA Fair Play coin

Badge refers to the referee's local association

Referees must be smartly turned out, with shirt tucked in at all times

Referees may carry a handkerchief in case players get dirt in their eyes

TOOLS OF THE TRADE
Certain items are vital to the referee's job. Red and yellow cards may seem like a long-established part of soccer but they were introduced only in the 1970s. It is believed the whistle was first used in 1878 and it was soon recognized as the best way of controlling play. Barrel-shaped whistles used to predominate but other shapes are now common. The referee carries a notebook and pencil to record details of the game and a special coin that is tossed to decide which team kicks off and in which direction.

THE REFEREE

WORKSOP

YOU'RE BOOKED

Bookings used to be given only once or twice per match and sendings off were extremely rare, but FIFA now insist that referees be much stricter. As a result, teams regularly have to play with 10 team members, or even fewer.

A red card is shown when a player has committed two bookable offenses

Cards are produced with a flourish from this pocket

The referee times the game with a watch

Referees have to be in shape to keep up with play on the field

Former USSR

Australia

New Zealand

Bangladesh

Iceland

Portugal

USA

Colombia

Italy

WORLD-CLASS REFEREES

These badges are produced by Referees' Associations around the world. Despite all the abuse they receive, referees are motivated by the prospect of officiating at top-class games. World Cup matches are controlled by officials from all countries affiliated to FIFA, not just those that qualify as competitors.

LINESMAN FIFA 82

LINESWOMAN FIFA 95

Official FIFA badges for sewing on the officials' shirts

Men and women officiate at top-level soccer games

TOUCHLINE HELPERS

The first linesmen waved a handkerchief to alert the referee. Assistant referees today use a flag. They wave the flag when a player is offside, when the ball is out of play, and when they have seen an infringement on the field.

The first referees wore knickers

Blazer with pockets for a stopwatch and notebook

HOW TO BE A REFEREE

This illustration from the cover of a 1906 book entitled *How to be a Referee* shows the typical referee's clothing of that period. After taking an exam, referees usually start out at amateur level. They are assessed regularly to ensure that standards remain high. Today's top referees are now professional. They earn good salaries for officiating top games.

The field

AT THE START OF A SEASON, players can look forward to playing their first game on a smooth green field. If a field is not looked after, it soon becomes muddy and uneven, especially if cold, wet weather sets in. Groundskeepers try to keep the fields in good condition with the help of new species of grass and good drainage. In many northern European countries, soccer takes a midwinter break during the worst conditions. Wealthy clubs may lay a completely new field between games, but millions of amateur players have to make do with whatever muddy or frozen land is available.

This Samuel Brandão painting of Rio de Janeiro shows soccer being played on a dirt field.

Patterns can be made when mowing the field

STREETS AHEAD
In the days before traffic became too heavy, street soccer was a popular pastime. Children learned close ball control and dribbling skills in confined spaces. They often used heaps of clothes or gateways as goalposts.

Groundskeepers preparing for a game during the 1953 English season

Jean-Pierre Papin playing for AC Milan, Italy, on a snow-covered field

PLAYING IN SNOW
In snowy weather, the field markings and the white soccer are hard to see and the ground is slippery. If the markings can be swept clear and the field is soft enough to take a stud, play can usually continue, using a more visible orange ball.

HOT STUFF
In countries where the weather is cold during the soccer season, many methods have been tried to prevent fields from freezing. Undersoil heating was first installed in England at Everton in 1958. Before undersoil heating became common, groundskeepers put straw down as insulation and lit fires in braziers to lift the air temperature. Today, large covers are sometimes used to protect fields.

SLOPES AND SHADE

Modern fields such as Preston, England, *(above)* are usually laid with camber, which means that they slope slightly down from the center circle to the touchlines. This helps to drain water away. When large stands are built, less air and light reach the grass, stunting its growth. This has been a problem at some stadiums, such as the San Siro in Milan, Italy.

PAMPERING THE FIELD

Modern field maintenance is a full-time job. In the summer, the grass must be mowed, watered, and fed regularly. During the close season, work is done to repair holes and worn patches in the turf. New types of grass have been developed that grow better in the shade of tall stands. This is vital in helping the groundskeepers to keep the field in good condition.

The surface is made to mimic grass

Fibers are woven together to form a carpet

Artificial grass viewed from the side, top, and underneath

BETTER THAN THE REAL THING?

Artificial fields are made from synthetic turf laid on a shock-absorbent pad. They are more hard-wearing than grass fields and are unaffected by torrential rain or freezing cold. Clubs with an artificial field can rent out their stadium for a range of events, such as concerts, and their home games need never be postponed because of bad weather. Many players do not like the surface because they feel that it increases the risk of injury.

Grass is kept long to encourage deep rooting

Layer of top soil nourishes the grass

Heating pipes laid in grids

Layers of sand and gravel allow water to filter away

The base of the field is composed of large pieces of stone

Drainage pipes carry away water

Model of a section through a field

SATURATION POINT

Rainwater is the greatest threat to field condition. Good built-in drainage is therefore an important part of field construction. Pipes and materials chosen for their good draining qualities are laid under the grass. A large amount of sand is mixed into the top soil to make it less absorbent and less prone to becoming waterlogged. Even a well-cared-for field may become saturated. Groundskeepers sometimes have to resort to using garden forks to remove standing water.

Soccer skills

Early 20th-century button showing a man heading the ball

Eᴀᴄʜ ᴘᴏsɪᴛɪᴏɴ ᴏɴ ᴛʜᴇ ꜰɪᴇʟᴅ is associated with a specific range of tasks. Defenders must be able to tackle the opposition and claim the ball, midfielders need to pass the ball accurately to their teammates, and strikers have to shoot and score goals. Although most players specialize in a certain position, professional players are expected to master a range of skills and work on any weaknesses. As part of their daily training routine, they practice hard to perfect their skills so that their technique does not let them down in a game.

CONTROL FREAK
The best players, like England's Wayne Rooney, can always bring the ball under control. To deal with high passes, players need to keep their eyes on the ball and use their chests, stomaches, heads or, like Rooney here, their thighs to stun the ball..

Shouting helps the players to pick each other out

TACKLE TALK
Players try to take the ball from another player by tackling. Lilian Thuram of France, playing here for Parma, Italy, is one of the world's great tacklers. He shows the timing and precision that are essential to avoid committing a foul. Referees punish players if they make a physical challenge from behind or if they make contact with a player instead of the ball.

Lilian Thuram

Hand signals are used to improve teamwork

Constant movement into space is essential

PASS MARK
Moving the ball quickly around the field, from one player to another, is the most effective means of stretching a defense. Accurate passing remains the hallmark of all successful teams. Zinédine Zidane was the star of the 1998 World Cup final for France. He had the vision to pass the ball into space for his strikers even when he was tightly marked.

If the defender is unable to reach the ball, he must still challenge the striker

The player must time his leap to meet the ball firmly

Oliver Bierhoff

All parts of the foot are used to manipulate the ball in the desired direction

One-touch passing of the ball is the hardest to defend

HEADS UP!
There are two distinct kinds of heading: defensive and attacking. Defenders try to gain distance when they clear a high ball out of the goal area. Attackers need accuracy and power to score goals with a header. Oliver Bierhoff of Germany, playing here for AC Milan, Italy, was an outstanding striker in the air.

The ability to pass with both feet gives the player more options

Leaning back helps to ensure that the ball will rise toward the top of the net

GOING FOR GOAL

When shooting, forwards need the accuracy to find the corner of the net as well as the power to blast the ball through the defense. Gabriel Batistuta of Argentina would beat goalkeepers regularly with his powerful right foot.

Keeping the head still improves accuracy

Keeping your weight over the ball makes it easier to cross with power

Extending the arms assists with balance

WINGING IT

Crosses, or passes in from the wings, result in more goals than any other angle of attack. Players who can put the ball over with pace and accuracy are extremely valuable to a team. David Beckham of England and Los Angeles Galaxy is renowned for the way he crosses from the right wing, curling the ball around the full-back and away from the goalkeeper. This type of swinging cross is often used when players are taking corners. They curl the ball in from the corner toward the goal and the waiting strikers.

The left leg is firmly planted to allow the body to make the best shape for the cross

The foot turns in as it passes through the ball to make it swerve

The player can feint to go in one direction before going in the other

The bicycle kick is even harder if the ball is moving across the player

DOWNTOWN DRIBBLER

When a player runs with the ball at his feet, it is called dribbling. Brazilian star Ronaldinho, who learned his soccer on the streets of Porto Alegre, is proof that dribbling can cause problems for the opposition. Good balance and concentration help a dribbler to change direction quickly and ride tackles.

BICYCLE KICK

The bicycle kick was first demonstrated in the 1930s by Brazilian forward Leonidas. It is one of the most difficult skills to pull off. With their back to the goal, strikers throw their legs up in the air and kick the ball while falling backward. This tactic sometimes catches the goalkeeper by surprise. This model of Italian striker Roberto Baggio shows the ideal body position.

A higher jump allows the player to keep the ball down below the crossbar

The goalkeeper

A 1900s Vesta, or match holder, showing a goalkeeper punching clear

As THE LAST LINE of defense, a goalkeeper knows that a single mistake can cost the team victory. Goalkeeping can be a lonely job. It entails having different skills from the rest of the team and you can be unoccupied for several minutes at a time. The recent change to the back-pass law, forcing the goalkeeper to kick clear rather than pick up the ball, has made the job even harder. The necessity of having both a physical presence and great agility means that goalkeepers have to train as hard as any other player, but the reward for this diligence can be a much longer career than that of their teammates.

Clothes

Until 1909, goalkeepers were distinguishable only by their cap, making it difficult for the referee to judge who, in a goalmouth scramble, was handling the ball. From 1909 to the early 1990s, they wore a shirt of a single plain color that was different from the shirts worn by the rest of their team. A rule forbidding short sleeves was made but has now been relaxed.

GOOD SAVE
This 1950 comic cover shows the save that is considered to be the easiest to make—from a shot straight to the midriff. It also hints at the spectacular action in which goalkeepers are regularly involved, such as when they have to fly through the air to tip the ball away. Modern strikers are likely to make the ball swerve suddenly, so it is all the more important for goalies to keep their bodies in line with the ball.

CATCH IT
Punching the ball away from the danger area has always been popular among European and South American goalkeepers. The goalkeeper depicted on this 1900 book cover is trying to punch the ball but he probably should be trying to catch it because he is not being closely challenged. In the modern game, referees rarely allow goalkeepers to be charged when they are attempting to catch the ball.

The ball should be punched out toward the wing

KEEPERS' COLORS
Patterns in soccer shirts have traditionally been limited to stripes and hoops but since the rules on goalkeepers' clothes were relaxed, every combination of colors seems to have been tried. Not all of them have been easy on the eye, although fluorescent designs are easy for defenders to see.

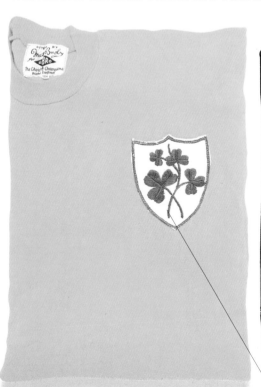

The shamrock, symbol of Ireland

EIRE SHIRT
This shirt was worn by Alan Kelly for the Republic of Ireland. He made 47 appearances, the first against West Germany in 1957 and the last against Norway in 1973. Yellow shirts were once a common sight in international games. Green was not an option for the Irish goalkeeper because the strip of the Irish team is green.

GOALIE'S GLOVES
Until the 1970s, gloves were worn only when it was wet, and they were made of thin cotton. Modern goalkeepers wear gloves in all conditions. Various coatings and pads are used to increase the gloves' grip, which is the key to handling the ball.

Flexible plastic ribs reinforce each finger

Modern gloves help to prevent injuries such as broken fingers

NARROWING THE ANGLE

This image from the 1930s shows a goalkeeper alert to danger. When an attacker approaches the goal with the ball, goalkeepers should leave their line and move toward the ball to reduce the target area for the attacker. This "narrowing of the angle" is an important part of keepers' roles. They often make marks, in line with the posts, to help them keep their bearings when leaving the line.

Most goalkeepers may still wear a cap if the sun is in their eyes

Arms are outstretched, ready to block a shot

THROWING OUT

This painted button from the 1900s shows one of the goalkeeper's jobs. A quick throw out, particularly after catching a corner, can be an effective way of launching an attack. Some goalkeepers are renowned for the length of their throw.

GOAL KICK

When the ball is put out behind the goal line by an attacker, the opposing team is awarded a goal kick. The goalkeeper takes the kick from inside the 6-yard (5.5-m) box. Early leather balls absorbed water and increased in weight, so a goal kick rarely reached the opposition's half.

LOUD AND CLEAR

Peter Schmeichel was famous for the vehemence of his reaction when a teammate made a mistake. Here he is shouting at Roy Keane when playing for Manchester United, England. Although such eruptions risk undermining team spirit, it is far better for goalkeepers to communicate with their defenders than to be quiet. Goalies also have to shout when organizing the wall at free kicks.

Tactics

PART OF SOCCER'S appeal is its tactical element. Coaches and managers try to outwit the opposition by keeping their tactics secret until the game. Since soccer first began, teams have lined up in different formations trying to play in a way that will take the other team by surprise and result in a goal. Early players had the physical attributes and skills needed for a particular position on the field. Today, the pace of the game demands that players be adaptable enough to play in almost any position, in the manner of the Dutch "total soccer" teams of the 1970s.

Old Arabic print of team formations

Center-half defended and attacked

2-3-5 formation (left)

Center-half only defended

W-M formation (right)

France won the 1998 World Cup with a back four

Wingers have been replaced by midfielders who can also defend

4-4-2 formation (right)

IN GOOD FORM (ABOVE)
The 2-3-5 formation dominated tactics until the 1930s. Each player had a very specific place and role on the field. Herbert Chapman of Arsenal, England, was the first manager to make a radical change, positioning the center-half and inside-forwards deeper to create the W-M formation.

GAME PLAN (ABOVE)
Managers use a board like this in the locker room. They use it to show players how to counteract the opposition and where they should be at certain points in the game. This is particularly important when defending corners and free kicks.

One forward often plays "in the hole" behind the other

Wing-backs are responsible for providing attacking width

Sweeper must be creative and pass accurately

Sweeper system (left)

CLEAN SWEEP
Modern formations are very varied, but the 4-4-2 is one of the most popular. The four defenders are not expected to push forward and the four midfielders sometimes switch to a diamond shape. The sweeper system, perfected by the Italians in the 1960s, frees one player from marking duties to act as cover.

The forward cannot go "one on one" with the goalkeeper

OFFSIDE ORIGINS
The first offside law, in 1866, stated that three defenders, including the goalkeeper, had to be between the attacker and the goal when the ball was being played forward by a teammate. By 1920, fewer and fewer goals were being scored because, even if attackers were onside at the vital point, they still had to beat the last outfield defender.

OFFSIDE UPDATED
In 1925, FIFA decided to amend the offside law so that only two players had to be between the attacker and the goal. Immediately, far more goals were scored. The offside rule is basically unchanged today. Here, the midfielder is about to pass the ball to the forward. This player is still onside and, once in possession of the ball, will have only the goalkeeper to beat.

Player is offside

OFFSIDE TRAP
Teams without a sweeper, like Norway under Egil Olsen, are still able to use an offside trap. As the midfielder prepares to pass the ball forward, the defenders suddenly advance up the field in a line, leaving the forward offside when the ball is played. William McCracken of Newcastle, England, was famous for first perfecting this tactic, in the years before World War I.

PACKED DEFENSE
Denial of space to the opposition forwards is vital and certain players may be singled out for man-to-man marking. It is often said that the best teams are built from the back, with a strong defense providing a springboard for attack. Here, several defenders are surrounding a striker.

The attacker is trapped

The defenders are physically blocking the attacker in

NO SUBSTITUTE
Substitutions were first allowed by FIFA in 1923, but only if a player was injured. Injuries were faked so often to let coaches make tactical changes that it was gradually accepted that one player could be freely replaced. Now the number of substitutes allowed per team has increased to five for some games.

BE PREPARED
Javier Zanetti's goal for Argentina against England at France '98 was an example of how a well-rehearsed routine can work brilliantly. Lots of goals are scored from set-pieces— movements that a team practices before a game. Coaches spend a great deal of time going through these with the team in training.

Injury time

Mr. Black, the player from a Happy Families game

A PROFESSIONAL PLAYER'S job involves far more than playing games and enjoying the limelight. Training, fitness, and recovery from injuries are day-to-day concerns for the modern player. Advances in medicine mean that injuries that a few years ago would have led to inevitable retirement can now be successfully treated. The pace of the modern game is unrelenting and loss of fitness is likely to stop a player from staying at the top level. Physiotherapy, nutrition, and even psychology are all parts of the conditioning program of big clubs today.

FIGHTING FIT
Medicine balls like this were used in soccer training for many decades. They are extremely heavy, so throwing them improves stamina and also builds muscle bulk. Sophisticated gym equipment, training programs, and resistance machines are now commonly used. Strength and fitness are essential to success in the modern game because top players have to play as many as 70 games per season. The greatest players are superb athletes as much as they are skilled players.

VITAL EDGE
Vittorio Pozzo, one of the first great managers, led Italy to victory in the World Cup in 1934 and 1938. He realized the importance of physical fitness and made his team train hard to give them a vital edge over their opponents. This paid off in overtime in the 1934 final, when Italy eventually scored the winning goal.

WARM UP AND COOL DOWN
A proper game-day routine can help to prolong a player's soccer career. Modern players are aware of the importance of warming up thoroughly before a game. The risk of muscle tears and strains is significantly reduced if the muscles are warm and loose. Recovery after games is also important. Many teams "warm down" after a game to relax their muscles before resting them.

The stretcher is carried by two wooden poles

A pillow is built into the stretcher

A piece of canvas supports the injured player

GETTING CARRIED AWAY
This stretcher was used in the 1920s. In those days, if the stretcher was brought out on the field, the crowd knew that a player was seriously injured. Today, players are given a few moments to get up before they are carried off to prevent time wasting and a delay to the game. They often run on again shortly afterward. In the US, motorized carts have taken the place of traditional stretchers.

AS IF BY MAGIC ...
The "magic" sponge has a special place in soccer folklore. Spectators have often wondered how a rubdown with a sponge and cold water could result in a player's swift recovery from an injury. Today, the team physiotherapist, rather than the trainer, treats players for injury problems on the field and off it. Physiotherapists are fully qualified to give sophisticated treatment to injured players.

The sponge is still used in amateur games

The physiotherapist carries plenty of equipment onto the field

Security pass

Modern medicine cases are light and waterproof

SOLDIERING ON
Injured players are usually substituted to prevent them from doing more damage, but some injuries do not need to stop a player from turning up for an important game. Paul Gascoigne, above, wore a plastic mask when playing for England against Poland in 1993, to protect a fractured cheekbone. During the 1978 World Cup final, Holland's Rene van der Kerkhof wore a cast on his hand.

FIELD DOCTOR
Nigeria's Daniel Amokachi is shown here being treated for a hamstring injury during a 1994 World Cup game. The hamstring muscle, at the back of the leg, is one of the most vulnerable for a player. Straining it usually results in a three to four week layoff.

Ice is applied to the injury to reduce inflammation

The bag is made of leather

LOTIONS AND POTIONS
This medicine bag belonged to Ramsgate FC in the early 20th century. It was a non-League team from Kent in England. The bottles would have contained various lotions and medicines to warm muscles, pour on grazes, or reduce pain. Professional clubs in many countries are now required to have a doctor on hand at every game to deal with serious head injuries and fractures.

The trainer's medicines sometimes included chloroform to sedate a badly injured player

Soccer balls

MUCH OF THE APPEAL of soccer lies in the fact that it can be played without any special equipment. Children everywhere know that a tin can, some bound-up rags, or a ball from a different sport entirely can be satisfyingly kicked around. This ingenuity was first displayed hundreds of years ago, when people discovered that an animal's bladder could be inflated and knotted to provide a light, bouncy ball. A bladder alone did not last very long when kicked, so people began to protect the bladders in a shell made of animal skin cured to turn it into leather. This design worked so well that it is still used today but with modern, synthetic materials rather than animal products.

An 1890s brass traveling inkwell in the shape of a soccer

HEAVY GOING

Balls of the 1870s were often formed by stitching together eight segments of leather, the ends of which were secured by a central disk. The leather was unprotected and could absorb water on wet days, so that the ball increased in weight. Heading the ball could be dangerous, even fatal, and so this technique was not often used in those days. The dribbling game was the popular style and the heavy ball was suitable for this style of play.

Manufacturers' names were first stenciled on balls in about 1900

Sections of leather sewn together

The lace for tightening the case stands proud

Interlocking panels of leather

Tool for lacing the ball tightly

Copper stencil

MADE TO MEASURE

This ball was used in March 1912, in the international match between Wales and England at Wrexham, Wales. England won the game 2–0. Made from a pig's bladder wrapped in cowhide, it is typical of the type of ball used for most of the 20th century. The outside shell was laced up. The size and weight of soccer balls were standardized for the first FA Challenge Cup competition in 1872, but the balls still absorbed water and were prone to losing their shape.

The colors are based on the French flag

Brand name marked on the ball with a stencil

WORLD CUP COLORS

The first World Cup balls to have a color other than black were used in the Finals in France in 1998. They had a shiny, synthetic coating to make them waterproof and incorporated a layer of foam between the latex bladder and polyester skin. This let players pass and shoot quickly and also put spin and swerve on the ball. Like 75 percent of the world's soccer balls, they were made in the Sialkot region of Pakistan.

HEADING FOR TROUBLE

Balls like this were used in the 1966 World Cup Finals, at which time ball design had hardly changed in 50 years. The leather case was backed with a lining, a development of the 1940s that improved durability. The outside was painted with a pigment that helped to repel some water from a rain-soaked field. Manufacturers had still not found a reliable alternative to lacing up the ball so players risked injury when they headed the ball.

The handle is pushed in to the cylinder to pump up the bladder

The piston expels air from the pump

The Nesthill brass pump

The sykometer measures air pressure

Pump is used when standing upright

Pressure valve

Pump from 1893 equipment catalog

Tube to attach the pump to the ball's valve

PATCHING THINGS UP
This 1970s repair kit would have been used with a vinyl ball. The metal rod was heated and then inserted into the puncture to create a hole of the right size, onto which a patch could be glued.

Pump is inserted straight into the ball

Patch with "nipple" to fit the hole

Glue

Spare valve

Metal rod

1630 engraving created by Matthaus Merian the Older

BALL BOYS
This 17th-century German engraving shows that inflated animal bladders have been used in ball games for a long time. The two men depicted are servants preparing a spare ball for their masters, who would have been playing pallone, a soccer-type game that was played in 17th-century northern Europe.

FULL OF AIR
Over time, air escaped from a ball's bladder and a pump was used to reinflate it. Sometimes, the air pressure in a bladder was increased to improve the bounce of the ball. If a bladder was pumped up too high it was likely to burst, so some pumps came with their own pressure gauge. These pumps date from about 1890.

The use of two colors makes the Orkney ball flash in the air

Calcio balls are made of leather that is stitched together and then painted

Alternative balls

Several different football games are played around the world today. They each use a ball particular to that game. Some of these games have existed for centuries. The balls may have features connected to a ceremonial aspect of the game, and involve decoration and color, or they may be designed to withstand harsh treatment. In some modern games the ball has evolved along with the game.

SHAPING UP
The game of American football was originally based on kicking a ball. As throwing became a central feature, the present shape of the ball evolved. The small ball can be gripped firmly, making it easier for the quarterback to make long, accurate passes.

COOPER
OFFICIAL
191

BUILT TO LAST
In the Scottish Orkney Isles, a type of football, or soccer, game is played through the streets every New Year. The ball is much heavier than a normal soccer ball and is stuffed tightly with pieces of cork. This helps it to last for several hours of play and also makes it float on water—a useful feature because a team can score a goal by throwing the ball into the sea.

MADE TO MATCH
Calcio, first played in Italy in the 16th century, was reintroduced to Florence in 1930. The game is played by teams of 27 a side, all wearing medieval clothes and armor. Balls of various colors are used including green, white, and red to match the costumes. Calcio balls are smaller than regular soccer balls, making it easier for the players to pick them up and throw them.

Soccer cleats

OF ALL SOCCER equipment, cleats, or boots, as they are sometimes known, have changed the most over the last 100 years. Always the most expensive item of gear, they remain an unaffordable luxury to many players around the world, who have to play in bare feet. The fast, agile sport we see today would simply not be possible if the heavy, cumbersome shoes worn up until the 1930s were still used. Professionals then dreaded having to "break in" hard, new boots, which involved a great deal of pain. They preferred to patch up an old pair again and again until they fell apart. In the first World Cup tournaments in the 1930s, the South American teams wore lighter, low-cut boots, much to the astonishment of the Europeans. These began the trend toward the modern, high-tech cleat.

A 1950s painting of soccer boots called *Christopher's Boots*, by Doris Brand

MULTIPURPOSE BOOTS
In the late 1800s, very few people playing soccer would have had special footwear. These girls' boots could also have been worn to school or in the house. The smooth soles, pronounced heel, and extremely high cut would have seriously constricted movement, but the ankle would have been well protected.

19th-century girls' boots

1920s child's boots

A "kick around" is a popular pastime with children

MADE FOR THE JOB
By the 1920s, soccer boots like the "Manfield Hotspur" were being mass-produced for players of all ages. Children's boots were designed just like adults', with reinforced toe caps and heels, some ankle protection, and leather studs, or cleats. Social conditions at the time, though, meant that most working-class families could not afford such equipment and, if they could, they would have handed down boots from one child to another.

STUDLESS BOOTS
A 19th-century gentleman player wore studless boots, which would not have allowed for sharp turns or long passing. However, they were practical enough for the type of dribbling game favored by the great English amateur teams like the Corinthians. This style of play was dictated by the confined spaces used for soccer practice at many British private schools. Boots like these would have doubled in weight when wet.

BOOTS IN THE BATH
In 1910 these boots were marketed as "Cup Final Specials," an early example of a soccer product being tied to a famous match. The wickerwork pattern on the toes was one of several designs that were thought to help a player control the ball—a major part of modern shoe design too. It was common for a player to wear a new pair of shoes in the bathtub for a few hours to soften the leather.

Extra foot support

Cotton laces

LOTS OF LACES
Paton's bootlaces, in various colors, were widely used from the 1930s onward. There was a constant demand for replacements because repeated soaking during games followed by drying out caused the early cotton laces to perish and eventually snap.

PERSONALIZED CLEATS
Cleats of a color other than black or brown are a feature of the modern game. Moustafa Hadji of Morocco was one of several players to wear a different color at the 1998 World Cup. However, they were not unknown in the past. Puma produced a white boot in 1958, and England player Alan Ball was known for his white cleats a decade later.

White laces were common in the 1930s

England's Tom Finney promoted these boots

THE MODERN LOOK
The classic black-with-white-trim design, which is still used today, began to be popular in the 1950s. The vertical strap on the instep remains from earlier designs. The cleats were becoming flexible enough to be worn without much breaking-in. There was less protection around the ankle, which allowed players more freedom of movement but led to an increase in injuries. It was at this time that shoemakers began to use the name of famous players to sell their products.

THE DESIGNER AGE
A vast amount of money is spent on the research and development of modern cleats. Top-quality leather uppers, usually made from kangaroo hides, and light, synthetic soles combine to make cleats that last. They are comfortable and allow the best players to put amazing amounts of spin on the ball. These cleats were specially designed for Brazilian star Ronaldinho and sold to the public with real gold applied to the logo.

Studs and stuff

The number of studs, or cleats, on the sole, and the way in which they are positioned, varies greatly. Longer cleats are needed if the field is wet and muddy; shorter ones are worn if the field is hard. The potential they have to cause injury has always been a concern to the game's governing bodies—in the 1930s, the wearing of illegal shoes was a sending-off offense. Since 1900, one of the jobs of the referee or an assistant has been to check the cleats of every player entering the field of play. Anybody wearing cleats with sharp edges or protruding nails is not allowed to play.

Wooden hammer

Nails fixed to cleats

Separate nails

Cleats are screwed into the sole

Key for tightening the cleats

THE FIRST CLEATS
Early soccer boots were made entirely of leather. The cleats had to be hammered into the soles.

HARMFUL HAMMERS
Rubber cleats came next. They also needed to be nailed to the sole and it was not long before the boots were damaged.

ALL CHANGE!
Modern screw-in cleats are made of plastic or metal. Players can change their cleats at half-time, to adjust to changes in conditions.

Soccer outfits

In the 19th century, both soccer and rugby players wore knee-length knickerbockers with no leg protection.

Shirts, shorts, and socks were described as the basis of a soccer player's outfit in the first Laws of 1863 and they remain so today. The materials used for a player's outfit have changed since then.

Players in South America and Mediterranean countries needed clothing suitable for warm climates, so wool gave way to cotton and then artificial fibers. Cool fabrics that "breathe" are now the norm worldwide. Teams wear matching outfits, or strips, on the field of play. The colors are the colors of the club, with which all the fans can identify. Most clubs and international sides have a home and an away strip in case two teams wear the same colors.

DUTCH ORANGE
The Holland uniform is unusual in being orange, and is recognized all around the world. The Dutch fans wear replica shirts and other orange clothes to form a mass of color at games. Here, Marc Overmars is on the ball for Holland during the 1998 World Cup Finals.

WOOL SWEATERS
In the late 19th century, soccer jerseys were often made from wool. They tended to stretch out of shape and could become heavy in the rain because they soaked up water.

AWAY UNIFORM
In the 1966 World Cup final, the England team wore cotton shirts with a round collar. Although England was playing at home, it did not wear its normal white home strip because West Germany was wearing white. Players wore red instead.

LACE-UPS
At all levels of the game, teams began to wear matching uniforms. This black-and-white shirt was worn by a member of Newcastle United's team for the 1908 English FA Cup final. Newcastle still wears black-and-white today. The shirt is made of thick cotton with a lace-up collar. Lace-up collars became fashionable again in the 1990s and were worn by Manchester United, among other teams.

AUSTRALIAN AMATEURS
This Australian shirt is made from wool with a cotton collar. It was worn in 1925 by the player Tommy Traynor. Shirts worn in international games have symbolic importance. At the end of the game, the teams swap shirts with each other in a gesture of goodwill.

KEEPING COOL
Today, most shirts are designed to keep players cool and draw away excess moisture. This 1994 Brazil World Cup shirt is made of light, synthetic fabrics. With the energetic pace of modern games, such improvements are vital, especially for games played in hot climates.

FAIR-WEATHER FRIENDS
By the early 20th century, manufacturers in many countries had begun to adapt the gear that British players had taken overseas with them in the 19th century. They produced lighter outfits more suited to warm climates. Short-sleeved shirts and deep V-neck collars became part of the typical Mediterranean look, as represented on this image from Valencia in Spain.

Early 1900s Spanish illustration

These socks are unusually decorative

Women were not expected to head the ball

PULL YOUR SOCKS UP
These socks from the 1920s look just the same as modern ones but they are made of wool. Modern socks are made of synthetic materials, making them more comfortable. Players keep up their socks with ties around the top. The ties can be made from strips of bandage or elasticated tape cut up into lengths. Toward the end of a grueling match, when players are prone to cramp, they may discard the tie-ups. Socks around the ankle can be a tell-tale sign of a tired soccer facing defeat.

Hoops and stripes are classic design features

High kicking was easier if shorts were above the knees

Cream flannel shorts from about 1900

Modern synthetic shorts with decorative side seams

Hard-wearing cotton shorts from the 1930s

Early 20th-century French illustration

SHORT STORY
Amateurs in the 1860s played in full-length pants but, as the game developed, players had to increase their speed and agility. Shorter knickerbockers cut just above the knee became popular. The baggy style of soccer shorts of the 1930s was made famous by Alex James of Arsenal, England, "the wee man in the big shorts." This fashion was revived in the 1990s following a trend in the 1970s and 1980s for tight shorts.

UNDER WRAPS
Until World War I, women players had to keep their hair under a cap or bonnet and hide their legs inside voluminous bloomers. In the 1910s, when many men were away at war, crowds flocked to see women's exhibition games. This wider acceptance of ladies' soccer enabled women's teams to start wearing soccer outfits that were similar to those worn by men and more suitable for the game.

Accessories

INJURY AND DISCOMFORT were part of the game of soccer in its early days. When protective equipment and other accessories, such as hats, ear muffs, and belts, were introduced at the end of the 19th century, they helped to distance the game from its rather violent past. Shin pads were developed in 1874 by Nottingham Forest's Samuel Widdowson in response to the physical punishment that players suffered during games. Leg protection is still part of gear today, but other accessories are no longer used.

LASTING DESIGN
In the 1900s, players would have worn shin pads like these outside their socks, held in place with straps and buckles. The front section is made of leather and the back of cotton, with a stuffing in between of animal hair. This mix of materials was used in shin pads until the 1960s.

Buttoned tunic was an alternative to the more common shirt

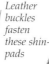

Leather buckles fasten these shin-pads

THE FIRST SHIN PADS
The earliest shin pads were worn outside the socks and were extended to include ankle protectors, which rested on the top of the shoe. Some, like these, had a suede covering, which was more prone to water damage than other types of leather. These heavy and inflexible pads date from the 1890s, about 20 years after shin pads became part of the player's gear.

REINFORCED GUARDS
This figure is from a picture on the box of a late 19th-century German soccer game. His shin pads, worn over the top of his socks and knickerbockers, appear to be strengthened with cane bars.

BELT UP
Decorative belts were a part of many schoolboys' soccer gear until the 20th century. They smartened up appearances by holding in the shirt and gave teams identity through the use of colors. Belts were also part of women's gear in the early 1900s.

Early 20th-century schoolboys' belts

Woman's belt from 1895

1980s shin pads were similar in shape to those from the 1930s

Long laces to wrap around the leg twice

ROOM TO MOVE
By 1910, ankle protection was no longer part of shin pad design, not because it was not needed, but because it restricted movement of the foot. Passing and running of the ball had become important parts of the game, requiring increased flexibility of the ankle. Players were therefore forced to sacrifice some protection. Cork was sometimes used to strengthen pads.

TIE-ON SHIN PADS
Shin pads worn inside the socks had taken over by 1930. Laces were used for fastening instead of buckles, to prevent chafing on the players' legs. Many years later, tighter-fitting synthetic, rather than woolen, socks held the pads firmly in position without the need for ties of any sort.

LIGHTWEIGHT PROTECTION
Modern shin pads look dramatically different from earlier models. They are shaped to fit the leg, using lightweight materials to give excellent protection. Even the delicate Achilles tendon at the back of the ankle is shielded. The revival of ankle protectors, after a gap of 100 years, brings shin pad design full circle.

KEEPING WARM
Gloves have become common, especially among players from hot countries who play in Europe, often in freezing temperatures. Players susceptible to hamstring and groin injuries are encouraged to wear undershorts because they help to keep these important muscles warm.

Ladies wore hats to keep long hair out of the mud

Stripes to match team colors

Women's soccer hats

SOCCER FIGURE
This porcelain figure of a boy was made in Germany in the 1890s. Artistic depictions of soccer from this period often showed players wearing hats, even though they were becoming decorative rather than practical items.

Hand-painted German figure

French soccer player Thierry Henry

HATS OFF!
These women's hats date from 1895, when ladies' soccer was still in its infancy. The fact that women played in hats does not mean that theirs was a gentler game. Like the men, many female players wore shin pads for protection.

Famous players

SOCCER IS A TEAM GAME. Clubs and national sides inspire the greatest passion among fans, but a few players are so gifted and entertaining that they stand out from their teammates and draw thousands of extra people to games. Some great players are famous for their spirit of fair play, while others have been surrounded by controversy and bad publicity. But all of the great players share an ability to change the course of a game through a moment of incredible individual skill.

GORDON BANKS (b. 1937)
English goalkeeper Gordon Banks is remembered for one save in particular—a spectacular effort that kept out Pele's header in the 1970 World Cup. Banks won 73 caps between 1963 and 1972 and would have won more, but for an eye injury.

JOHANN CRUYFF (b. 1947)
One of the few great players also to have become a successful manager, Cruyff was able to instill in his teams some of the style and tactical awareness that made him such a joy to watch. He played for Holland, Ajax, and Barcelona, Spain. He personified the concept of "total soccer" by floating all over the field and using his amazing balance and skill to open up defenses.

GERD MULLER (b. 1945)
Known as "Der Bomber", Gerd Muller was an unlikely looking center-forward. He had an astonishing spring in his heels, which made up for his lack of height. He was a prolific goal scorer, with 68 goals in 62 games for West Germany. Most of his club soccer was played with Bayern Munich, Germany, for whom he scored a record 365 goals.

Milla was a great entertainer, known for his flamboyant goal celebrations

Roger Milla after scoring for Cameroon against Colombia in the 1990 World Cup

ROGER MILLA (b. 1952)
Twice African player of the year, Roger Milla of Cameroon was the first player to become famous worldwide playing for an African country. He was also the oldest player to appear and score in a World Cup Finals in 1994, aged 42.

BOBBY CHARLTON (b. 1937)
Manchester United star Bobby Charlton survived the Munich air crash that killed eight of his teammates in 1958. Known for the power and accuracy of his shooting, he was invaluable in England's 1966 World Cup win. He was knighted in 1994.

Eusebio practices ball control in training

Eusebio scored 38 goals in 46 internationals

EUSEBIO (b. 1942)
Although he was born in Mozambique, Eusebio was snapped up by Benfica of Lisbon, Portugal, and went on to play for Portugal, in common with several other talented players. He starred in the 1962 European Cup final, scoring twice as Benfica beat Real Madrid, Spain, 5–3. Eusebio was respected all over the world for his fair play and dignity, as well as for his talent.

Meazza (below right) shakes hands with Hungarian captain, Sarosi, before the 1938 World Cup final

COUPE DU MONDE 1938

GIUSEPPE MEAZZA (b. 1910)
Italian Giuseppe Meazza won two World Cup winner's medals in 1934 and 1938. He was respected as a creator and scorer of goals from his inside-forward position. In 1938, he organized the Italian team when the coach, Pozzo, was ordered to leave the bench and sit in the stands. He spent his best years at Internazionale of Milan, Italy, and won 53 caps.

DIEGO MARADONA (b. 1960)
Maradona was the best player of his generation and also one of the most controversial. He had a tremendous ability to inspire his teammates, most notably when leading Argentina to the 1986 World Cup and Napoli to two Serie A titles in Italy in the late 1980s. His magical left foot and strength in possession were his main assets.

Maradona's low center of gravity gave him excellent balance

In the 1986 World Cup against England, Maradona scored two goals—one a handball that should have been disallowed, the other a dazzling solo effort

Like many of the greatest players, Maradona liked to be number 10

GARRINCHA (b. 1933)
Nicknamed "the Little Bird," Garrincha had polio as a child. He overcame his disability to become one of the quickest and most elusive wingers the game has seen. He played on the right-hand side of Brazil's legendary 1958 forward line. In 1962, he made up for the absence of the injured Pele with some brilliant performances, helping Brazil to retain the World Cup.

Maradona's magical footwork entertained and amazed the fans

Continued on next page

MARCO VAN BASTEN (b. 1964)
Van Basten of Holland scored one of the greatest goals of all time at the European Championship final in 1988—a volley from wide of the goal. Sadly, an ankle injury cut short his career.

LUIS SUAREZ (b. 1935)
Considered one of the best-ever Spanish players, Luis Suarez dominated the midfield for Barcelona, Spain, in the late 1950s. By the mid-1960s, he was playing a key part in Italian Inter Milan's new *catenaccio* system—a line-up heavy on defense with only two forward players. He was famous for his fast breaks out of defense and accurate passes. Suarez went on to be manager of Spain at the 1990 World Cup.

Kopa was the greatest French player of the 1950s

Kopa was known for his careful ball control and well-thought-out passing

Van Basten was the best center-forward of the late 1980s

RAYMOND KOPA (b. 1931)
Creative midfielder Raymond Kopa made his name with French club, Reims. He led the club to the first European Cup final in 1956, where it lost to Spain's Real Madrid. Kopa played for France at the 1958 World Cup and was named European Footballer of the Year in 1959.

The two defenders are playing for the Italian club Roma

Roma defenders are left in Platini's wake

STANLEY MATTHEWS (b. 1915)
England's Stanley Matthews was known for his dribbling skills. One of his finest performances was in Blackpool's 4–3 win over Bolton in the 1953 English FA Cup final. He won 84 caps and played his last game for Stoke City at the age of 50. He was knighted in 1965.

LEV YASHIN (b. 1929)
Always dressed in black, Lev Yashin was rivaled only by Gordon Banks as the greatest goalkeeper of his era. He played for the Soviet Union in three World Cups and is, to this day, the only goalkeeper to have been named European Footballer of the Year.

Between them, Puskas and Di Stefano scored seven goals in the European Cup final in 1960

FRANZ BECKENBAUER (b. 1945)

Beckenbauer's intelligence shone on the field as he dictated play from a deep sweeper position. Together with Johann Cruyff, he is one of the few soccer-playing legends to achieve similar success as a manager. Having captained West Germany at the 1974 World Cup, he managed the team when it won again in 1990.

FERENC PUSKAS (b. 1927)

The star of Hungary's famous team of the 1950s, Ferenc Puskas was part of the Hungarian team that beat England 6–3 at Wembley in 1953. He joined Real Madrid of Spain in 1958. Puskas strongly favored his left foot, scoring a wealth of stunning goals for both club and country.

ALFREDO DI STEFANO (b. 1926)

When Real Madrid dominated European soccer in the 1950s, Di Stefano was one of its star players. His stamina enabled him to contribute all over the field. He and Puskas formed one of soccer's legendary double acts.

MICHEL PLATINI (b. 1955)

Platini was one of those players who seemed happy to take the weight of a nation's expectations on his shoulders. He captained France in the 1984 European Championships, and France won the tournament for the first time. Platini was an attacking midfielder who often finished as top scorer at Italian club Juventus.

Michel Platini playing for Juventus

Platini had the speed and foresight to move forward into space

PELE (b. 1940)

Many people's choice of the greatest player of all, Pele was king of Brazilian soccer from the late 1950s to early 1970s. He overcame constant fouling by frustrated defenders to score more than 1,000 goals for Brazilian club Santos, American soccer team New York Cosmos, and the Brazilian national team. His enthusiasm and obvious love of playing, despite being plagued by injury, make him a perfect role model for the game of soccer.

Medals and caps

IT IS THE GOAL OF ALL soccer players to play well and win each game. Those lucky enough to win a championship are awarded a medal as a mark of their achievement. Those good enough to be picked to play for their country win a cap. Medals and caps have been part of the game since the 19th century and are still highly valued rewards today. At the highest level, success can be measured by the number of caps a player has and passing the "100 cap" mark is considered exceptional service to the national team. Thomas Ravelli of Sweden won 138 caps—a record for a European.

Argentine pot made from a dried eggplant trimmed with silver

Ornate silver dagger

Norwegian silver spoon

Argentine silver spoon

Medals

As with military medals for soldiers, players are rewarded with medals for helping their side, not for a moment of personal glory. Medals are awarded at all levels of soccer, professional and amateur. They are mementos by which players can remember their glory days and can become valuable collectors' items.

GOOD SPORT
Before organized leagues were established, soccer medals were often awarded for sportsmanship as well as victories. The fullback C Duckworth was given this medal for "gentlemanly and successful play" in the 1883–84 season.

WITH COMPLIMENTS
This "complimentary medal for defeating all comers" was awarded in the 1884–85 season.

PRECIOUS GIFTS
As well as caps and medals, international players are sometimes presented with gifts by opposing soccer associations. The England team members each received a silver spoon when they faced Norway in 1949. The Argentine FA gave the English team members ceremonial daggers and other silver items on their first visit to Wembley, England, in 1951.

English v Scottish League 1893

FA Cup runner-up 1893

DOUBLE
This group of medals belonged to R. H. Howarth of the Preston North End "Invincibles." The team won the League and the FA Cup in 1888–89, achieving the first English "double."

Lancashire Cup winners 1887

TROPHY TRIUMPH
This plaque was made to commemorate an international game between France and England in 1947. All the English players received a plaque after winning the match 3–0.

CLUB STRIKERS
Some clubs strike their own medals to mark a special achievement of their players. This medal was awarded at the end of a season to players of a team that had won its league.

HUNGARY FOR SUCCESS
Hungary was one of the first continental European countries to take to soccer. It copied the way other countries organized the game, including the awarding of medals. This medal was awarded to the members of an international side after a game against Austria in 1909.

1909 Hungarian medal

CHAMPIONS
This medal was awarded to a player for success in the 1914–15 season.

AMATEUR
This 1920s medal was given to a successful amateur player.

ARSENAL STAR
This 1930s medal may have belonged to soccer star Alex James.

Caps

A colored cap was once the only way of showing to which side a player belonged. In 1872, the FA ruled that teams should wear distinctive shirts. In 1886, it was suggested that caps be awarded to players each time they played for their country. Today, they are given to every member of a national team, including playing substitutes. Often, only one cap is awarded for a series of games so a player with 50 "caps" may have fewer actual ones.

HOME CAP
This Welsh cap was awarded for the 1903–04 Home International games between England, Scotland, Northern Ireland, and Wales. This tournament took place every year until 1984.

CAREY'S CAP
The great defender Johnny Carey won this cap when he played for Ireland against Poland and Switzerland in 1938. Carey won 36 caps.

Tassels are added for decoration

Welsh national crest—a dragon

1903-4

Details of games can be embroidered into each panel

The date covers games from a whole season

Northern Ireland had its own team from 1921

Soccer caps are usually made from velvet

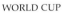

SCHOOL COLORS
Soccer caps were first awarded in English private schools. "Colors," in the form of caps, were given to the most able players in each year.

IN TRAINING
It is not only players who are rewarded for their efforts. Trainer Will Scott received this medal when the English and Scottish Leagues met at Celtic Park, Glasgow, Scotland in November 1931.

WAR GAMES
Throughout World War II, famous international players took part in exhibition games arranged to boost public morale. In 1946, Tom Finney was given this set of three medals after appearing in a game in Antwerp, Belgium.

PROMOTIONAL MEDAL
By the 1950s, businesses had started to commemorate a range of soccer events. The French newspaper, *Le Soir,* made this medal to mark a club tour of Austria in 1953.

WORLD CUP
The biggest achievement in soccer is to win the World Cup. This is a spare Jules Rimet medal from the 1954 final, when West Germany beat the favorites, Hungary.

AFRICAN CUP
This medal was presented to the winners of the first African Nations' Cup in 1957. The competition was held in Khartoum, Sudan, and only Sudan, Ethiopia, and Egypt took part. Egypt beat Ethiopia 4–0 in the final.

Famous clubs

ITALIAN ZEBRAS
Juventus is the most successful Italian club and enjoys great support outside Turin. Nicknamed the Zebras for their black-and-white striped uniform, they won the European Cup in 1985 and 1996.

CLUBS INSPIRE the greatest loyalty and passion from soccer fans, more so even than national teams. In every country, certain big clubs attract followers from beyond their local areas and tend to dominate their domestic leagues and cups. Success for these clubs often continues because financial backing ensures a steady supply of good new players. In all corners of the world, people swear allegiance to Barcelona or Liverpool, Flamengo or Milan, although they may never be able to attend a game involving their team.

BRAVO BENFICA
Only Porto and Sporting Lisbon rival Benfica in the Portuguese League. Benfica has also had some notable victories on the more competitive European stage. Benfica was the great team of the early 1960s, winning two European Cups, in 1961 and 1962, and reaching but losing three further finals.

This bronze depicts Benfica's symbol, an eagle

Figure of the ancient Greek hero Ajax forms the basis of the Dutch club's crest

MIGHTY MARSEILLE
In 1993, Marseille, led by the attacking threat of Allen Boksic and Rudi Voller, beat AC Milan of Italy 1–0 to lift the European Cup. French administrators, such as long-time FIFA President Jules Rimet, have always had a large role in soccer but it was 1993 before a French team won a European trophy.

LONDON LADIES
Netty Honeyball was the force behind the first great women's team in the 1890s. The British Ladies Club drew large crowds for its exhibition matches in London at a time when the capital was lagging behind the North and Midlands of England with regard to soccer.

YOUNG TALENT
In the 1970s, Dutch club Ajax's policy to develop its own young players bore fruit. The players, including the star Johann Cruyff, helped Ajax to three consecutive European Cup wins in the 1970s and some of them helped the national team in two World Cups. Despite regularly selling its best players, the club returned to the forefront of European soccer in the mid-1990s.

The club Ajax was formed in Amsterdam in 1900

BUSBY BABES
English club Manchester United started life as Newton Heath. It changed its name in 1902. The Munich air disaster of 1958, in which eight of manager Matt Busby's young team died, inspired sympathy around the world. Since then, the club has won two European Cups—in 1968 and 1999.

Baines card from the 1890s shows fullback Jack Powell.

PLAY UP NEWTON HEATH

POWELL

J. BAINES LITH. MANNINGHAM

THE GOLDEN YEARS
Bayern Munich followed Ajax as the leading European team in the early 1970s. It won three consecutive European Cups with the help of players such as Franz Beckenbauer, Gerd Muller, and Sepp Maier, who were also important to the German national team.

Paul Breitner of Bayern Munich in 1974

Dominguez, the goalkeeper— from Argentina

Alfredo di Stefano, the leader of the team

Francisco Gento, the fast left winger

REAL RIVALRY
In the late 1950s, Real Madrid, Spain, possibly had the greatest club side ever. Legends such as Di Stefano and Puskas inspired this Spanish team to win the first five European Cups. Real Madrid has a spectacular stadium—the Bernabeu—and a bitter rivalry with Barcelona.

THE RED DEVILS
This picture shows the players Cagna and Rios of Independiente, Argentina, in 1995. In 1964, Independiente was the first Argentine club to win the South American club competition, the Copa Libertadores. The "Red Devils" went on to win the competition four more times between 1972 and 1975.

The fans

GONE BANANAS
In England in the late 1980s, there was a craze for taking large inflatables to games. Fans waved bananas, fish, and fried eggs in the crowd to show their support for their teams.

FOR ALL THE talent displayed by the players on the field, it is the fans who have made soccer the biggest game in the world. From the last years of the 19th century, working people began to have enough free time to attend sporting events. They created an atmosphere of excitement and expectation, and large crowds became an important part of a game. Today, soccer is the most widely watched sport in the world. Fans are more eager than ever to show their support for club and country in a range of noisy and colorful ways.

Manchester City, England, pennant

Preston North End, England, rosette

PERFECT VIEW
In their desperation to see a game, fans are not always put off by the "ground full" signs. In the 19th century, before large-scale stands were built, trees provided a convenient spot from which to watch a popular game.

CLUB COLORS
Colors are a vital part of the bond between a team and its supporters. Once, people made rosettes for big matches and displayed pennants. Now, fans often wear a scarf to show their loyalty.

Holland scarf

Lazio, Italy, scarf

RARE COLLECTION
Fans have always collected objects bearing images of soccer. Today, the items probably feature their favorite club but, in the past, designs were based on more general soccer scenes. Collecting autographs is also a popular hobby and offers a rare opportunity to meet star players.

Jack Rowley, forward

John Aston, fullback

Johnny Carey, fullback

Matt Busby, manager

Child's piggy bank

1950s autograph book containing signatures of famous figures of Manchester United, England

Wooden pencil case

During World War II, the sound of the bell warned people of an air raid

Air-raid patrolman's rattle

Air-raid patrolman's bell

Adult's rattle

Rattles were originally used as bird scarers

Top section moves around and around horizontally

"Rattling" noise created at the handle

NOISY SUPPORT

Rattles were part of the atmosphere at games until the 1960s. When the horizontal section of the rattle is whirled around the "clicker" on the handle, it produces a loud rattling noise. Since the 1960s, organized chanting has become more common. Modern safety regulations restrict what items may be taken into the stadium, and rattles are no longer allowed.

Child's rattle

Child's rattle painted with a soccer scene

WAR CRY

Fans have taken bells and rattles to matches to express their support since before 1940. This bell and rattle were part of an air-raid patrolman's equipment in England during World War II. In 1946, after the war, a Derby County fan took them to games during Derby's run-up to the English FA Cup final.

WORLD FAMOUS

Brazilian fans were famous for their noisy support long before the rest of the world discovered paint and drums. They produce a samba beat on their drums and blow their whistles. As the noise echoes around the stands, the fans dance to accompany the action, especially if their team is winning.

AFRICAN PAINTING

Face painting has become commonplace at major international games, adding to the color and spectacle of the occasion. Here, two Zambian fans, painted to reflect the team's colors, enjoy an African Nations Cup match. Face painting is particularly popular with Dutch, Danish, and Japanese fans.

Game day

This is a Scoreboard from an early 20th-century French soccer game.

THE ATMOSPHERE of a big game, the sound of the crowd, and the closeness of the players combine to make going to a live soccer game very addictive. Even though soccer is now widely shown on television, millions of fans still go to the games. Many supporters, like players, are extremely superstitious and follow the same routine every time they go to a game. The crowd and the noisy support they give their team are essential to the game of soccer. It is vital that clubs continue to improve comfort and safety for their fans, so that they keep on coming back.

ALL DRESSED UP
This photo shows fans of West Ham, England, preparing to travel to the 1923 FA Cup final, the first to be held at Wembley. Many more than the official attendance of 123,000 crammed into the stadium. Notice the stylish appearance of the fans.

In the 1988 European Championship final, Holland beat the Soviet Union 2–0

Holograms and complicated designs are now used to deter ticket forgeries

TICKETS PLEASE
Tickets are essential in controlling access to games and keeping attendance to a safe level. Years ago, this was only necessary at cup finals and World Cup gamees. Tickets were issued for general areas in the stadium. Now that general seating being phased out in favor of ticketed seating, each game ticket corresponds to a particular seat.

READING MATTER
The earliest programs were simple one-sheet items, giving only team line-ups. As soccer became more popular, further elements were added, such as a message from the manager and background information on the opposition. Glossy, full-color brochures, largely paid for by advertising, are produced for tournaments such as the European Championships.

LET ME ENTERTAIN YOU
To make going to a game even more enjoyable, particularly for a family audience, clubs and governing bodies put on extra entertainment before kickoff and at halftime. In the past, this may have been in the form of a band, but modern crowds expect something more elaborate. The opening ceremony at Germany '06 featured Bavarian drummers and dancers lowered from the roof to the field.

A FAMILY AFFAIR
In the US, a trip to a sports event is often a family day out, and the stadiums have good facilities for everyone. There is a lot of razzmatazz at the Major League Soccer games. Cheerleaders and music keep the crowds entertained. This is game day at the Kansas City Wizards' stadium.

1903 FA official's badge

Official badge from 1905

The badges are made of cloth and decorated with gold brocade

FA badge from 1898

The English three lions motif

ACCESS ALL AREAS?
Away from the mass of spectators, there are certain areas of the stadium, such as the boardroom, where access is strictly controlled. These badges, from 1898–1905, would have been sewn on blazers and worn by Football Association officials. These days, executive boxes have become a feature of many stadiums.

Badge worn at 1899 England vs. Scotland international

CROWD CONTROL
Police and guards attend soccer gamees to ensure the safety of everyone at the game. Police, like these Italian officers at a Juventus game, may need to take a hard line with unruly fans, and sometimes use horses or dogs to help them control large crowds. They may also control traffic and escort supporters to and from the game.

COMING HOME
This drawing comes from a postcard from the early 20th century. The caption on the card says, "Our team's lost by ….. goals to …..". Space is left on the card for fans to fill in the score. Somehow, the depression of defeat is always replaced by excitement and high hopes when the next game comes around.

The stadium

WEMBLEY TOWERS
The famous towers at Wembley Stadium in England are sadly not part of the new 21st-century stadium.

As CROWDS GREW EVER larger in the late 19th century, soccer clubs realized that they would have to build somewhere permanent to hold their gamees. Stadiums became a necessity. They provided fans with shelter and a decent view of the game. They also created an atmosphere that added greatly to the game-day experience. A series of stadium disasters over the years, in places such as Scotland, Peru, and Russia, finally led to widespread belief that open seating should be replaced by stands for the safety of spectators.

SHEFFIELD WEDNESDAY F.C.

THEN THERE WAS LIGHT...
Floodlights were first used in 1878 but they did not become standard at professional clubs until the 1950s. The most common form of stadium lighting was on tall pylons in the corners of the stadium. Today, lights are often placed in rows along the stand roof.

CROWD SAFETY
On April 15, 1989, the FA Cup semifinal at Hillsborough, Sheffield, was the scene of the worst disaster in English soccer history. Ninety-six Liverpool fans died as a result of a crowd crush. The report into the tragedy began a major leap forward in stadium safety, to prevent a similar disaster from ever happening again.

STATE OF THE ART
The new Wembley Stadium in North London took much longer than anticipated to erect and construction costs were considerably higher than initial estimates. Once it opened, however, the public flocked to this stunning stadium with its 90,000 capacity and giant screens, each the size of 600 television sets. The stadium boasts a fantastic steel arch that is lit up at night and can be seen all across the city.

Lights along the top of the roof

STANDING TALLER
Barcelona, Spain, moved from Les Corts Stadium to the spectacular Nou Camp in 1957. Improvements for the 1982 World Cup and 1992 Olympics have increased the staggering height of the stands. The Nou Camp was paid for by the club's members.

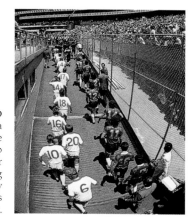

PATH TO THE FIELD
The tunnel is more than just a route on to the field. It is the place where players psych themselves up for the game and give in to their superstitions. Many insist on taking the same place in the line every time. Others put on their shirts only at the last moment.

The roof "hangs" from this crossbar

The pylon is integral to the structure of the stand

KEEPING UP TO DATE

Modern stands are designed using computer models to ensure that everybody has a good view. The space between seats is a difficult issue. More space means greater comfort, but it reduces the capacity of the stand. Designs, such as faces, are often picked out in the seats.

FANS ON THEIR FEET

Before all-seater stadiums were introduced, fans stood packed together in open seating. Far more fans could get in to watch a game and it is how the majority of people have watched games for much of soccer's history. Children were often passed over the heads of the crowd to the front to give them a better view.

WORLD CUP WONDER

The Stade de France is in St. Denis, north of Paris. It was built for the 1998 World Cup and 80,000 spectators watched the opening game there between Brazil and Scotland. The stadium was widely praised for its dramatic design. The roof, enclosing the ground in a continuous curve, creates an amphitheater effect, which has always been popular in European and South American stadiums.

Several tiers of seats

Field level openings for emergency vehicles

Revolving advertising billboards around the field

The World Cup

THE SOCCER WORLD CUP is one of the greatest sporting events of our time. The first World Cup was held in Uruguay in 1930, 26 years after FIFA first discussed the idea. In the early days, some teams were unable to travel to the host country but, by the 1950s, long-distance travel was becoming much easier and quicker. As the tournament became more accessible, it grew in popularity. The 1950 World Cup Final at the Maracana Stadium in Rio de Janeiro was attended by 200,000 people. In 1958, Brazilian teenager Pele became the first global soccer superstar. Since then, interest in the World Cup has boomed.

MANY MASCOTS
Every World Cup since 1966 has had a mascot. They appear as a life-size figure at games and scaled-down promotional or commercial images. This is Pique, from Mexico '86.

WORLD FIRST
Uruguay offered to pay travel and accommodation expenses to the 13 visiting teams at the first World Cup. Only four European teams made the long journey, joining the seven South American teams.

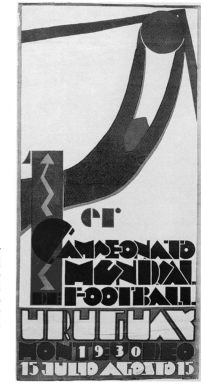

1954—Switzerland. West Germany beat Hungary 3–2 in one of the great upsets in World Cup history.

1958—Sweden. Brazil beat Sweden 5–2. Brazil is the only team to have played in every Finals tournament.

1950—Brazil. Uruguay beat Brazil 2–1, in the first tournament after World War II.

1962—Chile. Brazil beat Czechoslovakia 3–1, with Garrincha taking center stage after Pele was injured.

1938—France. Italy beat Hungary 4–2, inspired by its star inside-forward, Meazza.

1966—England. West Germany lost 2–4 to England in overtime, with Geoff Hurst scoring the first hat trick in a final.

1934—Italy. Czechoslovakia lost 1–2 to Italy. Uruguay did not defend its crown, the only time this has happened.

1970—Mexico. Brazil beat Italy 4–1 and was one of the greatest teams of all time.

1930—Uruguay. Beating Argentina 4–2, Uruguay was the first of many host countries to win the Cup.

1974—West Germany. Holland was beaten 2–1 by West Germany, which came back from being a goal behind.

VARIOUS VENUES
Competition to stage the World Cup Finals is always fierce because it brings visitors and publicity to the host country. The 2002 Finals, in Japan and South Korea, were the first shared tournament. Brazil beat Germany 2–0 in the final.

Argentina '78 is remembered for the ticker tape in the River Plate Stadium

Mexico was the first country to host two Finals

The Italia '90 mascot was called Ciao

1978—Argentina. Holland lost 1–3 to Argentina, leaving the Dutch as the best team never to have won the World Cup.

1982—Spain. Italy beat West Germany 3–1, its striker Paolo Rossi finishing as leading scorer.

1986—Mexico. Argentina beat West Germany 3–2, in a tournament dominated by Diego Maradona.

1990—Italy. West Germany beat Argentina 1–0 in a defensive, bad-tempered final.

1998—France. Brazil was beaten 3–0 by France in an amazingly one-sided match.

1994—USA. Brazil beat Italy 3–2 on penalties after a 0–0 draw and became the only team to have won four World Cups.

The figure is a winged seraph

In 1994, American fans turned out in force to watch the games

The fans at Italia '90 provided more drama than some of the games

WANDERING TROPHY
The first World Cup trophy was designed by a French sculptor, Abel Lafleur. Originally named "Victory", it was later named in honor of the president of FIFA, Jules Rimet. The trophy was stolen before the 1966 tournament in England and was found in a park by a dog called Pickles. Brazil was presented with the trophy to keep in 1970 but, in 1983, it was stolen again and has not been seen since.

The trophy is made of solid gold

Sweden, the host team, made it to the final in 1958 but was overpowered by the Brazilian superteam

The World Championship in Football 1958
Sweden 8–29 6

STOCKHOLM

GÖTEBORG

HÄLSINGBORG
MALMÖ

Coupe Jules Rimet

READ ALL ABOUT IT
Programs for the World Cup are different from the club variety, in that they usually cover the whole tournament rather than a specific game. They contain information about the competing teams and are printed in several languages. These programs are from Sweden '58, England '66, Spain '82, Italy '90, and USA '94.

The engraving on the trophy is in French

COUPE DU MONDE
DE
FOOTBALL
ASSOCIATION
—
COUPE
JULES RIMET

Jules Rimet trophy

Garrincha

Didi

Pele was 17 in 1958

THE BEAUTIFUL GAME
The 1958 final saw Brazil emerge as one of the World Cup's greatest-ever teams. Their forward line-up was among the strongest in the game's history. Garrincha, Didi, Vava, Pele, and Zagalo drove the team to victory. Mario Zagalo later became the national team manager and was in charge when Brazil won again in 1970 and 1994.

Vava played at center-forward

Zagalo, the left-winger, scored the fourth goal in the final

Continued on next page

WE MUST HAVE THE WORLD CUP
This was the poster for the 1962 Finals in Chile. A series of earthquakes marred the run-up to the tournament but the hosts were determined. President of the Chilean FA, Carlos Dittborn, said "We have nothing. That is why we must have the World Cup." Chile overcame the doubts of some European teams by staging a successful event. There was more trouble on the field than off it, particularly in the "Battle of Santiago" between Italy and Chile. Italy finished the game with nine men.

Globe forms the top of the trophy

World Cup Willie inspired a World Cup theme song by Lonnie Donegan

The Union Jack flag represents Great Britain, not just England

Designed by Italian Silvio Gazzaniga, the trophy is made of solid 18-carat gold

The real trophy is 20 in (50.8 cm) high and weighs 20 lbs (9 kg)

World Cup Willie was a lion, inspired by the three lions on the England gear

Replica of the World Cup trophy

MASCOTS FOR MONEY
World Cup Willie was the first World Cup mascot. Designed for the 1966 tournament in England, he represented the increase in commercialism. Since then tournament mascots, such as Ciao of Italy '90 and Footix of France '98, have appeared on official posters and been sold in many forms.

NEW LOOK CUP
The present World Cup trophy was made for the 1974 Finals in West Germany. Having won for the third time in 1970, Brazil had been allowed to keep the Jules Rimet trophy for good. The new trophy was commissioned by FIFA, despite an offer from Brazil to provide a trophy named after FIFA president Sir Stanley Rous.

Argentina '78

THINKING POSITIVELY

In 1978, host Argentina inspired passionate fans with its positive attitude. The star of its winning team was Mario Kempes, who played club soccer in Europe.

ENTHUSIASTIC AMERICA

Despite having no strong tradition of professional soccer, the US hosted a successful World Cup Finals in 1994. Large and enthusiastic crowds attended all the games. This is a ticket for the game between Italy and Mexico, played at the former RFK Stadium, now the Jack Kent Cooke Stadium, home to football team the Washington Redskins.

Spanish Football Federation crest

Information pack for Spain 1982

A pack of cards illustrating the stadiums

HARD WORK FOR HOSTS

A country bids to hold the World Cup several years in advance. It tries to convince FIFA that it will be able to stage a successful tournament. It has to produce information about all aspects of the tournament, including the stadiums, transportation networks, accommodation, and media facilities.

The balls are brightly colored for the benefit of TV audiences

Each ball contains a slip of paper with a team written on it

WHO PLAYS WHOM?

Plastic balls like these are used to make the draw for the World Cup Finals. It is a fair way to decide who plays whom. The number of competing teams has steadily increased from 13 in 1930 to 32 in 2006. The present system ensures that every team gets to play three games in the first round. Then, for the rest of the tournament, games are played on a knock-out basis, until only two remain for the grand final.

IN THE BAG

This bag is a promotional item for the 2002 World Cup, staged jointly by Japan and South Korea. It was the first shared tournament and the first one held in Asia. Demand is sure to increase for smaller countries to benefit from this arrangement.

ZIDANE SEES RED

The defining moment of the 2006 World Cup final came when referee Orazio Elizondo sent off French captain Zinédine Zidane after his infamous head-butt of Italian defender Marco Matarazzi. With the score at 0–0 after overtime, Italy went on to win the game on penalties.

Cups and trophies

THE MOMENT WHEN a team captain is presented with a trophy and holds it up to the fans is the crowning glory of any campaign. Cups and trophies are the marks of success and the managers of many modern clubs know that, if they are to hold on to their job, their team has to win a competition. For clubs like Real Madrid in Spain, Benfica in Portugal, and Bayern Munich in Germany, finishing as runner-up is considered a failure. The desire to make money has led to the creation of many new competitions in recent years, some of which do not have the same prestige as older tournaments such as the European Cup or the Copa America.

TEAM TALK
The European Cup was originally for the champions of each country's league. Now the top two clubs compete. The competition was first held in 1956. At the 1985 final at the Heysel Stadium in Brussels, Belgium, 39 people died. A safety wall collapsed as fans of Juventus, Italy, and Liverpool, England, fought each other.

Program for the 1985 European Cup final

Corner flags used as decoration

EARLY CUP
This decorative, silver-plated trophy from the 1870s is an example of an early soccer cup. After the FA Cup was started in 1872, local tournaments for small clubs began to be set up all over England and Scotland along the same lines.

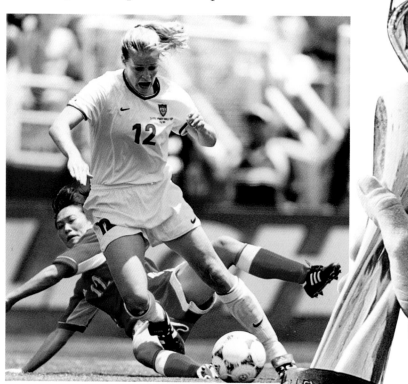

FULL HOUSE
In the 1999 Women's World Cup in the US, teams played in front of capacity crowds. The final was held in the Rose Bowl in Pasadena, California. Here, US player Cindy Parlow rides a tackle in the final against China. The US won, to secure its second World Cup victory.

WOMEN'S WORLD CUP
The first Women's World Cup took place in China in 1991. The final was held in Guangzhou, where the US beat Norway 2–1. The tournament went from strength to strength and the next two events, in 1995 and 1999, drew large crowds. This is the trophy awarded to the US in 1999.

The gold-plated Women's World Cup trophy has a soccer at the top

Holding the trophy aloft is a proud moment

LITTLE TIN IDOLS
The first FA Cup, on the left, was known as the Little Tin Idol. It was stolen from a store window in 1895 and was never recovered. The present FA Cup, on the right, was made in Bradford, England, in 1911.

PLAYER'S CIGARETTES

PLAYER'S CIGARETTES

ASSOCIATION CUP WINNERS
THE OLD CUP

ASSOCIATION CUP W
THE PRESENT CU

The silver UEFA trophy is decorated with men playing soccer

Names of previous winners engraved around the base

FROM STRENGTH TO STRENGTH
The African Nations Cup has been held every two years since 1957. It has grown from humble beginnings and as many as 16 teams now take part. Egyptian striker Hassan Hossam is pictured here after his team's 1998 triumph over the defending champions, South Africa. This was Egypt's fourth African Nations title.

COPA AMERICA CUP
First held in 1910, the Copa America is the oldest major international competition. It was originally played for only by South American countries but, in recent years, Mexico and the US have also taken part. Uruguay won the first official Copa America in 1917 and, along with Argentina, has been the most successful teams over the years. Brazil has not always played its strongest team. Since 1987, the tournament has been held every two years.

SECOND BEST
The UEFA (Union of European Soccer Associations) Cup was originally known as the Inter City Fairs Cup. The first competition was played over three years, beginning in 1955. Barcelona beat London 8–2 in the two-legged final. When the European Cup Winners' Cup was abolished in 1999, only two European club competitions remained. The strongest sides qualify for the European Cup and the next best play in the UEFA Cup.

The Copa America was conceived by Chile, Uruguay, Brazil, and Argentina

Playing the game

Two lead "kicking" figures from the early 20th century

This game was advanced for its time

GENERATIONS OF children have had their first contact with soccer, or "football," through toys such as blow soccer, card games, and Subbuteo. The popularity of soccer means that, as with other merchandise, there is money to be made from developing new products with a soccer theme. This drives manufacturers and inventors to come up with a vast range of games based on soccer, far more than on any other sport. The simplicity of the toys from the past, shown here, contrasts sharply with the speed and excitement of modern computer games. Today, children and adults can experience virtual soccer games and act out the roles of their favorite players and teams on play stations and in computer games.

Points are lost if a marble is trapped here

Marbles are fired up this chute

BALL ROLLING
This handheld toy was made in the early 20th century. It involves rolling the ball-bearing into one of the small holes.

IN THE TRENCHES
Trench Soccer was produced for British soldiers fighting in World War I. The player must move a ball bearing safely past the German generals to score.

SOCCER MATCHBOX
This is the world's smallest soccer game, probably made in Japan in the 1930s for small children. When the matchbox is opened, a spring is released, and the players leap up.

PINBALL
In this bagatelle game from the 1950s, players shoot marbles around the board using a spring in the bottom right-hand corner. Points are scored or lost according to where the marbles stop.

Ball for the
Kick game

Downward
pressure on
one leg causes
the other leg
to kick

The cards
feature
different
positions and
parts of the
game

KICK FIGURES
These figures come from a
tabletop game called Kick,
made in about 1900. A green
cloth field and goals with nets
are included. Players make
the mechanical players kick
by pressing them down on
the table. They are moved
around by hand—a
feature also used in more
modern soccer toys.

Combination of
red and white is
a classic soccer
uniform

Key fits
into the
ball to
wind it
up

SNAP!
This rare pack of early 20th-
century cards from an English
game of snap features soccer
characters. In snap, players aim
to collect all the cards. They turn
over cards until two identical ones
turn up together. The first player
to shout "Snap!" takes the pile.

WIND-UP PLAYER
This tin-plate wind-up
toy was made in Germany
in the early 1950s. When
wound up with a key, the
figure moves forward, as
if dribbling the ball. The
shirt, with its loosely laced
neck, is typical of the style
of soccer clothes worn in
Europe at that time.

CHAMPIONS!
This game, called
Championship
Soccer, was made in
1983. It uses two of
the classic components
of many board games—
dice and cards—to govern
the movement of
the ball around the field.
A scoreboard and clock
are also included.

QUICK CHANGE
These wooden blocks, with a
different picture on each side,
can be mixed up to make a
character. The shin pads and
ball reflect the style of the time
when the toy was made—1895.

Memorabilia

1910 silver Vesta (match holder) advertising the mustard maker Colman's

SOCCER appeals to all parts of the community, regardless of age or sex. The game can therefore be used to promote a wide range of items. Soccer-related advertising and product promotion is not a new phenomenon. In fact, companies were already latching on to the game's popularity in the early part of the 20th century. An understated style and original artwork predominated until the 1950s. This has been largely replaced today by mass-produced items, heavily reliant on star players and wealthy clubs.

Bank Top White Star

Welsh national team

Scottish club, Hearts

Chadderton, a non-league team

Wednesday, now Sheffield Wednesday

BAINES CARDS
These cards, produced in the late 19th and early 20th century, were the forerunners of sticker albums and other collectibles. They featured soccer and rugby league teams at professional and amateur level and had advertisements on the reverse side.

SPORTS TIN
By the 1930s, original artwork on a sporting theme was often used as a decoration for everyday household items. This tin features soccer on the lid and other sports, including cricket and hockey, around the outside.

Covered stands are rare in southern Europe

FIFA logo for Italia '90

SOUVENIRS
Mementos of the World Cup Finals do not stop at programs and tickets. There is great demand around the world for anything tied to the tournament, such as these erasers from Italia '90.

SOCCER FAN
This is a Spanish lady's fan from the mid-20th century. Printed in Barcelona, it has a soccer image on one side and carries a promotional message on the reverse. Many commercial objects of this period were designed to be artistic as well as functional.

POSTER PAINTING
In this advertising card of the 1920s an Italian drinks company has illustrated its product in a soccer scene, instead of putting a soccer image on the actual bottle.

HEALTHY KICK
There is no magic ingredient in this drink, but the images would have appealed to soccer fans. The manufacturers knew that any association with soccer would improve sales.

This label comes from a fruity soft drink. It was marketed as an ideal refreshment for half-time

This label implies that the drink will promote the robust strength that a soccerer enjoys

Class B17
locomotive

Name plate

Banks Johnstone Jennings England Best

TEAM TRAIN
In the early 1980s, the Hornby toy company of Liverpool, England, produced a series of these scale models of the London North Eastern Railway's locomotives, named after soccer clubs. This one is called the *Manchester United*. Real trains are also sometimes named after clubs.

PETROL HEADS
The Cleveland Petrol company produced these miniatures of British international players in 1971. The set was given away free with petrol sales.

The kicking leg is the second-hand

Pocket watch

Watch

Alarm clock

FULL TIME
This group includes a Swiss pocket watch made in Geneva around 1910, a British watch from the 1950s, and a more modern 1970s alarm clock. Design, materials, and therefore cost were dictated by whether the object was aimed at children or adults.

CHAIN MEDALS
Soccer items are often turned into jewelry and other personal effects. Four silver medals, struck in the 1920s, are attached to this chain. The silver locket and compass are from the 1880s.

Chain

Locket

Compass

Further medals could be added to the chain

OLYMPIC CLOCK
This German wooden clock may well have been made to commemorate the 1936 Berlin Olympics, where the soccer tournament was won by Italy, when it beat Austria 2–1 in the final. The figures at the top of the clock move on the hour.

The figure is the same on both halves

SOAP ON A ROPE
The Avon company produced this soap soccer to mark the 1966 World Cup Finals in England.

STRING ALONG
Made in the 1880s, this copper string holder prevents string from getting tangled. The string is pulled through a hole in the top.

CHOCOLATE
Melted chocolate would have been poured into this early 20th-century brass mold and left to cool and set, producing a miniature chocolate player with a ball at his feet. This item was made to appeal mainly to children and the general soccer theme would have been enough to make it popular.

The business of soccer

SOCCER IS BIG BUSINESS—fans attend matches in large numbers, club products sell worldwide, and top players and managers earn an incredibly large salary. The people who started professionalism in the 1880s realized the financial possibilities of soccer but, for many decades, the game carried on at much the same level. It provided cheap entertainment for the paying public and offered a decent living to players and managers. All that has changed now, as club owners and star players stretch soccer's money-making potential to the limit.

Gullit, pictured here in a preseason friendly game, occasionally played for the teams he was managing as player-manager

The emblem of the sponsoring local brewery

Even shin pads, worn under the socks, are marked with the name of the manufacturer

BILLY'S BRIBE
This shirt was worn by Welshman Billy Meredith, the greatest player of his era. As a player for Manchester City, England, he was banned from playing for a year in 1905. He allegedly tried to bribe the Aston Villa captain to lose an important game. This was the first major scandal of British soccer.

SHIRTS OFF
Replica shirts are a major source of income for professional clubs like England's Manchester United and Spain's Real Madrid. Three or four designs are now available at one time and new ones are brought out at regular intervals. Clubs produce hundreds of different products— from calendars to baby clothes; from candy to bicycles. These can be sold to fans all over the world, reducing the club's reliance on ticket sales.

MANAGEMENT STRESS
Managers are subjected to great stress in the modern game and have to accept that their every decision will be examined by the media. In most of the major leagues, the length of time allowed for a manager to produce a winning team can be measured in months rather than years. In 1999, Ruud Gullit was forced out of his job as manager at England's Newcastle United after just a few unsuccessful months.

SHIRT AD
Companies have been paying soccer clubs to put their logos on their shirts since the 1970s. The only club not to have a sponsor's logo has been the Spanish club, Barcelona. In 2006, the club carried the emblem of UNICEF—the United Nations Children's Fund—for free.

Strikers, such as Papin, fetch the highest prices

Papin's shirt advertises a French supermarket

MILLION-DOLLAR MAN
Jean-Pierre Papin became the first $15 million player, when he moved from Marseille, France, to AC Milan, Italy, in 1992. Since then, prices have continued to skyrocket, with Italian Christian Vieri joining Inter Milan from Lazio, Italy, for $50 million in 1999. Players today are eager to move regularly because of the signing bonuses they receive. Clubs often make record signings, even when they are heavily in debt.

Players who come from abroad, like Di Matteo, are in the majority at Chelsea, England

ALL ABROAD!
Political and legal changes have made it easy for player to move abroad and play for foreign clubs. European Union residents can now play in any member state. Roberto di Matteo was one of the first Italians to transfer abroad to an English club in 1996. Since then, a ruling has established that a club does not have to pay for a player whose contract has expired.

GROUND FORCE
Advertising in and around soccer grounds was allowed long before shirt sponsorship. In the 1950s, it featured mainly local firms, but now larger multinational companies exploit the exposure provided by television coverage. Some billboards rotate, to catch the eye of the watching public and allow more advertisers to use limited space. In some competitions, such as the European Champions' League, the same products are advertised at every game in the tournament.

Badge showing AC Milan's club logo

Brand logos are clearly visible on cleats

MEDIA MOGULS
AC Milan are one of the many teams with links to big business. Italian media mogul Silvio Berlusconi bought the club at a time when television coverage of the game was increasing. He was able to maximize commercial opportunities and attract star players from abroad.

World Club Cup

WORLD CHAMPIONS
The World Club Cup is contested by the winners of the UEFA Champions League and the Copa Libertadores. The first competition was between Real Madrid, Spain, and Penarol, Uruguay, in 1960. Originally a home-and-away fixture, won by the team with the highest aggregate score, it was changed in 1980 to one match only, played in Japan.

The science of soccer

FOR MANY YEARS, SOCCER was not considered a subject of scientific investigation and coaches and players relied largely on knowledge gained from experience. As technology has become more sophisticated, and the difference between winning and losing smaller, ways of using science to improve soccer have been developed. Nutritionists have transformed players' diets, physicists have studied how and why some players can bend the ball, and information technology has made a statistical analysis of the game possible.

BIOLOGICAL DIFFERENCES
For much of the first century of soccer, women were marginalized on the grounds that they were physically unsuited to the game. However, as the Brazilian player Milene Dominguez shows here, women have all the touch and skills of men, if not the sheer bulk and strength.

ISOTONIC NUTRITION
Players can lose up to seven pints of water during a game so it is imperative that they rehydrate their bodies during and after a game. Isotonic drinks, which contain a small amount of salts and sugars, are the most effective for doing this. The drinks also help replenish the player's stock of calories.

German players exercise their abductor muscles, which lift the leg outward from the body

Players run around poles to test their capacity to change direction at speed

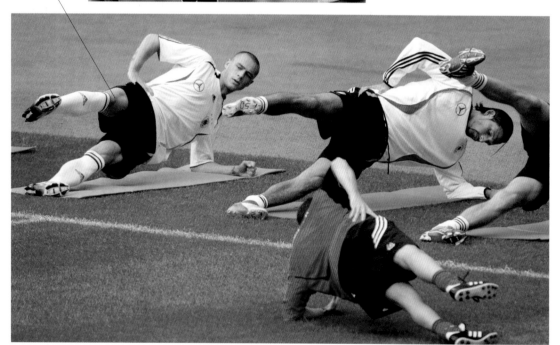

With one foot off the ground, turning on the run, players develop their sense of balance

TRAINING MUSCLES
Training was once little more than a few laps around the field, but today advances in medical science have resulted in highly specialized regimes. Players warm up and warm down to avoid muscle strain and do specific work on individual muscles to help them cope with the range of moves needed during the game.

The muscles in a player's leg have to learn to switch rapidly from relaxed to contracted and back again

PHYSICAL DEMANDS
The German national team was put through its paces before the 2006 World Cup, its levels of fitness monitored and recorded in training exercises like this.

A microchip inside the ball will determine whether the ball crossed the line

A CLEVER LITTLE CHIP
Did all of the ball cross all of the line? It is a question referees, players, and fans are always arguing over. The insertion of a microchip into this foam-stuffed ball, combined with field-side tracking devices, may one day provide a definitive answer.

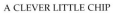

◁———— Direction of attack

Distance covered: 5478

PROZONE
New software—like Prozone—can track the precise movements of players in a game, recreate passages of play in animated form, and provide incredibly detailed statistics. This screen shows the movements of a central midfielder over one half of a game. The dot in the center shows the player's average position on the field while the distance the player has run is calculated at over 3 miles (5 km).

FLAGS THAT GO BLEEP
Assistant referees are now equipped with blip flags. If something has been missed, especially incidents off the ball, the assistant can alert the referee by pressing a button on the flag's handle. The referee's receiver, strapped to their arm, will then vibrate or bleep.

Flags with blip buttons like this were first introduced in the late 1990s

Did you know?

AMAZING FACTS

On average, each player in a game has the ball for only three minutes, the time it takes to boil an egg!

A three-minute egg

In 1965, substitutes were allowed for the first time, but only when a player was injured. Substitutes featured in the World Cup for the first time in 1970.

Luis Chilavert, goalkeeper for Paraguay, rushed out of his goal and scored for his team in a game against Argentina in 1998. The final score was 1–1.

The first person to score from a penalty in a World Cup final was Johan Neeskens for Holland in 1974.

In the 1994 World Cup finals, Russia failed to qualify for the later stages even though it scored more goals in the first stage of the competition than any other team.

The referee for the 1930 World Cup final wore a shirt, tie, jacket, and knickerbockers!

Johann Cruyff 's mother was a cleaner for the club Ajax in Holland. When she persuaded them to give her 10-year-old son a trial, they signed him as a youth player. He went on to be an international soccer star.

The goal net only became compulsory in 1892. The crossbar was introduced in 1875.

The first time teams used numbered shirts in an FA Cup final was in 1933. Everton wore numbers one to eleven, and Manchester City wore numbers twelve to 22.

Eight of the players who won the World Cup for Brazil in 1958 were in the team that retained the World Cup in 1962.

Only seven different countries have been World Cup champions, although there have been 18 finals.

The FA Cup is the oldest competition in soccer. The highest scoring FA Cup victory was on October 15, 1887, when Preston North End beat Hyde United 26–0 in the first round of the competition. The score was 12–0 at half time and 25–0 at 90 minutes. The final goal was scored in the five minutes of extratime added by the referee.

Tony Adams of Arsenal with the FA Cup

Pele scored 1,283 goals in his senior career.

Half of the world's registered soccer players are from Asia. Hide Nakata is one of the first Japanese players to make a career outside his country.

Hide Nakata

After Brazil had beaten Italy 4–1 in the 1970 World Cup final, reporters pursued Pele into the locker rooms and interviewed him while he had a shower!

Uruguay, with a population of just 3 million, is the smallest nation to have won the World Cup.

The first international soccer game played by a side with 12 players was in 1952, between France and Northern Ireland. One of the French players was injured and substituted, but after treatment he continued playing, and no one noticed until half time.

Two pairs of brothers, John and Mel Charles and Len and Ivor Allchurch, played in the Welsh team that beat Northern Ireland 3–2 in 1955. John Charles scored a hat-trick.

QUESTIONS AND ANSWERS

Q How many women play soccer in the US?

A Soccer is the most popular women's sport in the US, with around eight million players. USA Women won the first World Cup in 1991 and won it again in 1999. It was Olympic Champion in 1996, and narrowly lost by a golden goal to Norway in the Olympic final in 2000.

Q Why was the first World Cup held in Uruguay?

A Uruguay, host nation of the first World Cup in 1930, offered to pay travel expenses for all the teams.

Q Were old soccer balls heavier than those used today?

A People make the mistake of thinking that old soccer balls were heavier than those used today. They were virtually the same weight, but today's balls have a special coating that stops the leather from absorbing moisture. Before this development soccer balls could absorb water freely and on wet days the ball could double in weight, often making it as heavy as 2 lb (1 kg).

Leather soccer ball

Q When were floodlights first used?

A The first recorded use of floodlights was at Bramall Lane, Sheffield, England, in 1878. The lamps were placed on wooden gantries and were powered by dynamos.

Mia Hamm

Q When were women banned from playing on the grounds of FA clubs?

A On December 26, 1920, over 53,000 spectators packed into Everton's Goodison Park to watch Dick Kerr Ladies play St. Helens Ladies. The FA, worried that the women's game was socially unacceptable, banned women from playing on FA club grounds in 1921. The ban was not lifted until 1970!

Q Which country was the first to be knocked out of a World Cup in a penalty shootout?

A Penalty shootouts were introduced into the World Cup finals in 1982 and in the semifinals West Germany knocked out France in a penalty shootout.

Q Who plays soccer in the Olympic Games?

A The national women's soccer teams compete in the Olympics, but for men it is the national Under-23 teams that take part.

Q Who was England's first black professional player?

A Arthur Wharton, originally from the Gold Coast (now Ghana), played for Preston North End as an amateur in the 1880s. He then went on to play as a professional for Rotherham Town, Sheffield United, and Stockport County. He was also a gifted sprinter and could run 100 yards (91 m) in 10 seconds.

Q Why have there been three different FA Cup trophies?

A The first trophy was stolen while on display in a Birmingham sports shop window, after Aston Villa's 1895 victory, so a second trophy, a replica of the first, was made. When Manchester United won the FA Cup in 1909, it made a copy of this second trophy for one of its directors. As a result, the FA withdrew this trophy and made the third and current FA Cup trophy. Manufactured in 1911, it bears no resemblance to the original 1872 trophy.

Q What has the phrase "back to square one" got to do with soccer?

A When the UK's BBC first broadcast soccer live on the radio in 1927, the *Radio Times* printed a diagram of the field, divided into numbered squares. When the ball was passed back to the goalkeeper, the commentators would say, "Back to square one".

BBC radio microphone

Q When was the first official women's soccer game?

A Netty Honeyball, secretary of the British Ladies Football Club, organized the first women's soccer game in 1895.

Record Breakers

⚽ Brazil has won the World Cup five times, more than any other country.

⚽ The oldest soccer club in the world is England's Sheffield FC. Formed in 1857, the club has always played nonleague soccer.

⚽ Lev Yashin (Russia) is the only goalkeeper who has been chosen as European Footballer of the Year.

⚽ In 1999, Manchester United became the first team to win the Triple of the Premier League, the FA Cup, and the European Champions League.

⚽ Real Madrid has won the European Champions League nine times, more than any other team.

⚽ In 1957, Stanley Matthews became the oldest player to play for England when he won his 84th international cap at the age of 42. He continued playing Division One soccer until he was 50 years old.

Stanley Matthews collector's card

Who's who?

SOCCER IS A GAME OF SPEED and skill, and there are many outstanding players. With international competitions like the FIFA World Cup™, extensive media coverage, and a transfer system that allows players to sign for clubs in other countries, players from all parts of the world can become household names. Referees can also build up a considerable reputation around the world. These pages contain some of the past and present players who are among the world's best.

Italian referee Pierluigi Collina

GOALKEEPERS

• SEPP MAIER, WEST GERMANY, B.2.28.44
The pinnacle of Maier's distinguished career was in 1974, when he won the European Cup with Bayern Munich, followed by the World Cup with West Germany. He played with Bayern Munich for a total of 19 years.

• PETER SHILTON, ENGLAND, B.9.18.49
Renowned for his fitness and perfectionism, Shilton made his senior England debut when he was only 20 years old. Over the next 21 years he played for his country 125 times.

• PETER SCHMEICHEL, DENMARK, B.11.18.63
Schmeichel moved to Manchester United in 1991, where he has won five league titles and two FA Cups. In his trademark "star" save, Schmeichel runs out, spreads his arms and legs wide, and jumps toward the striker.

• DINO ZOFF, ITALY, B.2.28.42
Tall and determined, Zoff was almost impossible to beat. He appeared 112 times for Italy between 1968 and 1983 and captained Italy when it won the World Cup in 1982. With club side Juventus he won six Italian League titles and the UEFA Cup.

Dino Zoff

DEFENDERS

• FRANCO BARESI, ITALY, B.5.8.60
The best sweeper in the world for much of the 1980s and 1990s, Baresi would bring the ball forward and join in attacks. He retired in 1997, having played more than 600 times for club team AC Milan during his 20-year career.

Franco Baresi

• MARCEL DESAILLY, FRANCE, B.9.7.68
Born in Accra, Ghana, Desailly moved to France when he was a child. In 1993 and 1994, he won the Champions Cup twice, first with Marseille, and then with AC Milan. Desailly played a vital role for the French national team when it won the 1998 World Cup and the European Championship in 2000.

• PAUL BREITNER, WEST GERMANY, B.9.5.51
An adventurous, skilled left back at Bayern Munich, Breitner moved forward to midfield on transferring to Real Madrid. He was relaxed and seemingly nerveless in big games.

• ROBERTO CARLOS DA SILVA, BRAZIL, B.4.10.73
A player of great skill, with a reputation for taking ferocious free kicks, Roberto Carlos entered the Brazilian national team after the 1994 World Cup. A runner-up in 1998, he won the World Cup in 2002. He joined Real Madrid in 1996, winning the Spanish league in his first season and the UEFA Champions League Final in his second.

• FERNANDO RUIZ HIERRO, SPAIN, B.3.23.68
A gifted central defender, Hierro's surefooted tackling helped Real Madrid to win the UEFA Champions League Finals in both 1998 and 2002.

• PAOLO MALDINI, ITALY, B.6.26.68
An attacking fullback and one of the best defenders in the world, Maldini has captained AC Milan and Italy, appearing for Italy more than 120 times.

Bobby Moore

• BOBBY MOORE, ENGLAND, B. 4.12.41
A gifted defender and an excellent captain, Bobby Moore led England to victory in the 1966 World Cup. He played for England 108 times, only missing 10 matches between 1962 and 1972.

• OSCAR RUGGERI, ARGENTINA, B.1.26.62
Ruggeri was the heart of the Argentine defense in the 1980s, and a World Cup-winner in Mexico in 1986. He captained his national side and won a total of 89 caps.

MIDFIELDERS

- LUIS FILIPE MADEIRA CAEIRO FIGO, PORTUGAL, B.114.72
Figo was a European champion at under-16 level in 1989, and a World Youth Cup-winner in 1991. He won the Portuguese Cup with Sporting Clube in 1995, and moved to Barcelona, where he captained them to the Spanish league title in 1998, before moving on to play for Real Madrid.

- PAUL GASCOIGNE, ENGLAND, B.5.27.67
An extremely gifted player who possessed excellent ball control and passing skills, Gascoigne's career was hampered by injuries. He was an important member of England's 1990 World Cup team.

- ALAIN GIRESSE, FRANCE, B.9.2.52
A skillful player with excellent technique, Giresse was at the heart of the French midfield at the World Cup finals in 1982 and for the 1984 European Championships.

Gheorghe Hagi

- GHEORGHE HAGI, ROMANIA, B.2.5.65
Romania's greatest-ever player, Hagi was a youth international at 15 and a full international at 18 years of age. An outstanding midfield presence, he went on to play in Romania, Spain, Italy, and Turkey.

- FRANK RIJKAARD, HOLLAND, B.9.30.62
Rijkaard made his debut for Holland at the age of 19. A universally admired and versatile player, he played midfield for Milan but central defense for Holland. He moved around Europe, playing for clubs in Holland, Portugal, Spain, and Italy.

- VITOR FERREIRA BARBOSA (RIVALDO), BRAZIL, B.19.4.74
A fast, attacking midfielder, Rivaldo has skillful ball control and excellent passing skills. A great creator of goals, he can shoot with either foot, and is often successful with unorthodox overhead shots. He was a key player in the Brazilian national squad in the 1990s and was awarded FIFA World Player of the Year in 1999.

- SOCRATES, BRAZIL, B.2.19.54
A player with tremendous balance and poise, Socrates made excellent passes, but also scored terrific goals. He studied to be a doctor before becoming a soccer player, and returned to medicine once his playing days were over.

- ZINÉDINE ZIDANE, FRANCE, B.6.23.72
An outstandingly skillful player, Zidane was voted Young Player of the Year in 1992. He scored two goals in his national debut for France. He was FIFA's World Player of the Year both in 1998 and in 2000. A creative and inspirational player who is composed and confident on the field, he scored two of his country's three goals against Brazil in the 1998 World Cup final in Paris, becoming a French national hero.

Socrates

FORWARDS

- ROBERTO BAGGIO, ITALY, B.2.18.67
A gifted goalscorer, Baggio helped Juventus win the UEFA Cup in 1993 and the league title in 1995. He was FIFA's World Player of the Year and European Footballer of the Year for 1993.

- GEORGE BEST, NORTHERN IRELAND, B.5.22.46
An amazingly gifted player, Best had brilliant ball skills and excellent balance. He was European Footballer of the Year in 1968. Many feel that he could have played at the highest level for a longer time, had the success of his club side, Manchester United, continued.

- KENNY DALGLISH, SCOTLAND, B.3.4.51
Dalglish was probably Scotland's greatest-ever player. His ball-control skills were excellent, and he was able to slice through a defense with his bold, accurate passes.

- THIERRY HENRY, FRANCE, B.8.17.77
A striker possessing terrific ball control, incredible pace, and clinical finishing, Henry was top goalscorer for France when it won the World Cup in 1998.

George Best

- RAUL GONZALEZ BLANCO, SPAIN, B.6.27.77
An extremely gifted player with a knack for being in the right place at the right time, Raul scores stunning goals, both with his head and his feet.

- RONALDO LUIS NAZARIO, BRAZIL, B.9.22.76
Ronaldo scored his first goal for Brazil when he was only 16 years of age. An exciting, inspirational striker, his speed and skill enable him to break through almost any defense. Ronaldo was FIFA's World Player of the Year in both 1996 and 1997.

- KARL-HEINZ RUMMENIGGE, WEST GERMANY, B.9.25.55
European Footballer of the Year in 1980 and 1981, Rummenigge was a formidable forward

capable of cutting through a team's defense. Between 1976 and 1986 he appeared 95 times for West Germany, scoring 45 goals.

- CHRISTIAN VIERI, ITALY, B.7.12.73
A fast, decisive striker, Vieri ended his first season with Madrid in 1998 as the Spanish league's top scorer, with 24 goals. He scored five more for Italy in the 1998 World Cup finals.

Thierry Henry

Find out more

THERE ARE MANY WAYS of getting more involved in the world of soccer. An important start is to find a club you want to support, and follow its performance. If you like to play yourself, you can join a team and take part in a local league. By visiting museums such as The National Soccer Hall of Fame, for example, you will find out about managers, coaches, and scouts as well as players, and will build up a picture of the world of soccer. The more you learn, the more you will enjoy the soccer fever surrounding the big competitions, such as the World Cup finals.

Bob Bishop was the Manchester United scout who discovered George Best, Sammy McIlroy, and many others in the 1960s and 1970s

USEFUL WEBSITES

- To find out about the Football Association: **www.thefa.com**
- For information on the World Cup: **www.fifa.com**
- For playing tips and video masterclasses: **http://news.bbc.co.uk/sport1/hi/football/skills**
- Excited about soccer in the United States? Then visit the home of Major League Soccer—be sure to check out the youth programs: **www.mlsnet.com**
- For US soccer scores, team information, photos, news, and tickets: **www.ussoccer.com**
- Want the latest scores plus up-to-the-minute headlines? Visit: **www.usatoday.com/sports/soccer/front.htm**
- For up-to-date soccer information: **http://news.bbc.co.uk/sport**

SUPPORT YOUR TEAM

Decide which team you want to support and start following its results. If you can, go to some games and start your own collection of programs. Watching the games and reading the programs you will soon become an expert on your team's players and management. You will learn about soccer rules and will have your own ideas on tactics, and how the team should be run. If you get a chance to go to an international game, you will meet soccer supporters from other parts of the world.

SOCCER SCOUTS

All big clubs have scouts who travel around looking for new talent, whether it be established players that the club can "buy," or gifted youth players. Outstanding young players will be asked to participate in a trial, and if they are successful, may be invited to join the club's training academy. Here they will receive a general education as well as intensive soccer training. If all goes well they will work up through the youth and reserve teams to play in the club's first-string team.

Italian fans cheer for their team

JOIN A TEAM
If you are eager to play the game, then join a school or local youth-club team. You will quickly find out whether you prefer defense, midfield, attack, or goalkeeping. Team coaches will help you master many techniques, such as marking, tackling, dribbling, and passing. Regular training and practice games will ensure you are in good shape and have the stamina to play strongly until the end of the game..

Good close ball control is essential, whether you play in an attacking position or in defense

Places to visit

NATIONAL SOCCER HALL OF FAME AND MUSEUM, ONFONTA, NEW YORK
www.soccerhall.org
Established in 1979, the National Soccer Hall of Fame has housed an extensive archive of memorabilia associated with soccer in the United States for almost 20 years. The star of the museum is the Kicks Zone, a hands-on, feet-on interactive area that lets kids and adults actually kick and head balls and play unique computer games as well. Test your skills and your strategy with speed dribbles, a header cage, animated "Kick It" games, power shots, the Wall, and three-on-three challenges. Computer kiosks throughout the museum let visitors test their knowledge of soccer skills and trivia. Make sure to wear your sneakers!

THE SOCCER HALL OF FAME AND MUSEUM, VAUGHN, ONTARIO, CANADA
(905) 264-9390
The museum displays many soccer treasures and a wall of inductees to the hall of fame.

D.C. UNITED MAJOR LEAGUE SOCCER
RFK STADIUM
WASHINGTON, D.C.
(202) 432-SEAT (7328)
You can watch pro soccer played by D.C. United, or by any of the other major league teams in the country. Along with D.C. United, the Eastern Conference teams include the Chicago Fire, Columbus Crew, Metrostars, and New England Revolution; in the Western Conference, look for the Colorado Rapids, Dallas Burn, Kansas City Wizards, Los Angeles Galaxy, and San Jose Earthquakes. Visit www.mlsnet.com to get the schedule for your team.

FIFA WORLD CUP
GERMANY 2006

© 2002 FIFA TM

In all FIFA competitions, a Fair Play Trophy is awarded to the team with the best behavior

FIFA
For the Good of the Game

FIFA FAIR PLAY

FIFA fair play logo, introduced in 1993

THE 2006 FIFA WORLD CUP™
In the summer of 2006 the FIFA World Cup finals took place in Germany. Thirty-two teams competed in a total of 64 games, which were played in twelve different cities around Germany, from Hamburg in the north to Munich in the south. Qualifying games to be among the teams in the finals took place around the world in the two years before 2006. Hundreds of thousands of fans gathered in Germany for the finals, and it was a proving ground for German mass transit, accommodations, and police.

Glossary

AFRICAN NATIONS CUP First won in 1957. African national teams compete for the trophy every two years.

AGENT The person who acts on behalf of a player in the arrangement of a transfer or a new contract.

ASSISTANT REFEREES Formerly known as linesmen, one covers each side of the field. They signal offside, throw-ins, fouls, and substitutions.

BOOK The referee books players when they have committed an offense. He shows players a yellow card and writes their names in his black book. Players are sent off if they receive two yellow cards in one game.

CAP Originally a hat awarded to those playing an international game. Players count their international appearances in caps.

COACH Runs the training program, working closely with the manager.

COPA AMERICA CUP First won in 1910. North and South American national teams compete for the trophy every two years.

CORNER KICK Awarded when one of the defending team has put the ball out of play over the goal line.

CROSS A pass made from either wing to a forward at the center of the field.

A referee's uniform

DEAD BALL KICK A kick from non-open play, such as a free kick or a corner kick.

DERBY A derby "game" is a game between two local rival teams.

DIRECT FREE KICK Awarded if a player kicks, trips, pushes, spits, or holds an opponent, or tackles the player rather than the ball. The person taking the free kick can shoot directly at the goal.

DIRECTORS The people who serve on a board to help run a club. Some put a lot of personal money into the club.

DRIBBLING Running with the ball while keeping it under close control.

EUROPEAN CUP First won in 1956, it is now known as the Champions League. The top clubs from the league of each European country compete for the trophy every year.

FA CUP First won in 1872. English league and non-league teams compete annually for the trophy.

FIFA (FÉDÉRATION INTERNATIONALE DE FOOTBALL ASSOCIATIONS) Formed in 1904. The world governing body of soccer, FIFA sets international rules, arbitrates between countries, and runs the World Cup.

FOOTBALL ASSOCIATION Formed in 1863. The governing body of English soccer arbitrates between clubs and disciplines players.

Using your chest to control the ball

FORMATION The arrangement of the players on the field. The coach or manager chooses the formation, and may change it during a game in response to the strengths or weaknesses of the opposition.

GIANT KILLER A team that beats a side believed to be of a much higher quality, and from a higher division.

GLOVES Worn by goalkeepers to protect their hands and to help them grip the ball.

GOAL KICK Awarded when the ball goes out of play over the goal line if it was last touched by the attacking team.

GROUNDSKEEPER The people who look after the stadium, the terraces, and the soccer field.

HANDBALL It is an offense to touch the ball with your hands arms during play.

HEADING A defensive header sends the ball upward, clearing it as far away as possible. An attacking header sends the ball downward, hopefully into the goal.

INDIRECT FREE KICK Awarded for dangerous play or for blocking an opponent. The player cannot score directly.

The white ball was introduced in 1951

KICKOFF The kicking of the ball from the center point of the field to start the game.

LAWS The 17 Laws of the Game approved by FIFA.

MANAGER The person who picks the team, plans tactics, motivates the players, and decides what to do in training.

MARKING Staying close to an opponent to prevent him from passing, shooting, or receiving the ball.

MASCOT A person, animal, or doll that is considered to bring good luck to a team. Mascots are also part of the increasing commercialization of soccer.

OFFSIDE When an attacking player receives a ball, two defenders including the goalkeeper have to be between the attacking player and the goal. Players are only penalized for being offside if they interfere with play or gain some advantage by being in that position.

ONE-TWO An attacking player passes the ball to an advanced teammate and runs on into a space. The ball is immediately returned, bypassing the defending player.

PENALTY AREA A box that stretches 18 yd (16.5 m) in front of and to either side of the goal.

PENALTY KICK A shot at the goal from the penalty spot. Awarded against a team that commits an offense in its own penalty area.

PENALTY SPOT The spot 14 yd (13m) in front of the goal. The ball is placed here to take a penalty.

A soccer card

PLAYER'S CIGARETTES

KICKING TO SWERVE THE BALL

PFA (THE PROFESSIONAL FOOTBALLERS' ASSOCIATION) The trade union of soccer professionals in England and Wales that protects and promotes the interests of players.

PHYSIOTHERAPIST The person who helps players recover from injuries, and who checks players to make sure that they are well enough for a game.

FIELD The field of play. In the early days the boundaries of the field were marked by a series of flags. The FA introduced the field markings we know today in 1902.

PROGRAM Provides information for the fans about the players of their team and of the opposition, as well as a message from the manager.

RATTLE Supporters took rattles into games until the 1960s, when they started to sing or chant instead. Today, rattles are forbidden.

RED CARD The referee holds up a red card to show that a player has to leave the field. Serious foul play or two bookable offenses results in a red card.

REFEREE The person who has authority for that game to enforce the Laws of the Game.

SCARF Each team has a scarf in its own colors. Fans often wear the scarf or their team's jersey when they go to games.

SCOUT A person employed by a team to look for talented new players.

SET PIECE Moves practiced by a team to take advantage of a dead-ball situation.

SHIN PADS Pads worn inside socks to protect the lower legs.

SHOOTING A kick toward the goal.

STANDS The areas where the supporters sit or stand around the field.

STRIP The shirt, shorts, and socks a team wears. Most teams have at least two different strips, a home uniform and an away uniform. A team uses its away uniform when there is a conflict of colors.

STUDS (OR CLEATS) Small rounded projections screwed into the sole of a soccer shoe. The referee or assistant referee checks all studs before play starts. Players use longer studs on a wet, muddy field.

SUPERSTITIONS Many players are deeply superstitious. For example, they may insist on wearing the same shirt number throughout their career. Paul Ince would only put his shirt on for a game when running out of the tunnel.

TACKLING Stopping an opponent who is in possession of the ball and removing the ball with your feet.

TACTICS Planned actions or movements to achieve an advantage over your opponents.

TERRACES Steps where people stood to watch a game before the advent of all-seater stadiums.

THROW-IN A way of restarting play when the ball goes over the touchline. Awarded to the opponent of the player who last touched the ball.

World Cup medal

UEFA CUP Originally known as the Inter City Fairs Cup. First won in 1958. Some of the best teams from each European country's national league compete for the trophy every year.

WARM-UP A routine of exercises to warm up all the muscles before the start of a game.

WHISTLE Used by the referee at the beginning and end of a game and to stop play when there is a foul.

WINGER A striker who plays particularly on one side of the field or the other.

WOMEN'S WORLD CUP First won in 1991. National women's teams compete for the trophy every four years.

WORLD CUP First won in 1930. National men's teams compete for the trophy every four years.

YELLOW CARD The referee holds up a yellow card to book a player.

The Unites States Women's soccer team, June 1998

Index

Acknowledgments

Dorling Kindersley would like to thank
Hugh Hornby, Rob Pratten, Lynsey Jones, and Mark Bushell at The National Football Museum for their help and patience; Stewart J. Wild for proofreading; Hilary Bird for the index; David Ekholm-JAlbum, Sunita Gahir, David Goldblatt, Susan St. Louis, Lisa Stock, and Bulent Yusuf for the clip art; Neville Graham, Sue Nicholson, & Susan St. Louis for the wall chart; & Margaret Parrish for Americanization.

The publishers would also like to thank the following for their kind permission to reproduce their photographs:

a=above; c=center; b=below; l=left; r=right; t=top; f=far; n=near

Action Plus: Glyn Kirk 13l, 16cl, 16br, 17tl, 21cr, 56clb; Matthew Clarke 17c; Neil Tingle 10br, 56–57; 62b..
Allsport: 32cl, 32br, 33tl, 33c; Ben Radford 56cr; Christopher Guibbaud 57tl; Claudio Villa 16bl; Clive Brunskill 14bl; David Cannon 17c, 51cr; David Leah 51c; Don Morley 16br; Hulton Getty 34bl; Jed Jacbsohn 50c; Michael Cooper 57c; Michael King 34–5bc; Scott R Indermaur 43tl; Vincent Laforet 50br.

Associated Press AP: Alastair Grant 65tr.
Bryan Horsnell: 42cl, 42cfl, 42cnl.
Colorsport: 11tr, 19r, 21br, 27tr, 28tr, 32bl, 39tr, 44–5b, 57tr, 62tl; Jerome Provost 39bc; Olympia 34br, 35tl.
Corbis UK Ltd: S Carmona 44clb; Alexandra Winkler 59tr.
Empics Ltd: 32tnr; Don Morley 35tr; Michael Steele 41bl, 41br; Neale Simpson 38cl; Peter Robinson 34tc, 47l, 57br; Topham Picturepoint 34bc, 35tl; Witters 32tr; Matthew Ashton 62–63; Jon Buckle 64–65; Laurence Griffiths 63tl, 63ca; Peter Robinson 61clb.
FIFA: 62cb; 62br.
Getty Images: 60ca, 60cr, 61tr; Shaun Botterill 60–61; David Cannon 61cla; Phil Cole 31crb; Jonathan Daniel 65br; Stu Forster 56bl, 56cra, 61br; Stuart Franklin/Bongarts 59br; Markus Gilliar – Pool/Bongarts 58–59c; Mike Hewitt 42br; Ross Kinnaird 58c; Thomas Lohnes/AFP 58clb; Clive Mason 17fclb; Paolo Nucci/WireImage 49bl; Pierre-Philipe Marcou/AFP 58tl; Gary M. Prior 60tr; Cesar Rangel/AFP Photo 27cra; Jamie Squire 57tcl.
Hulton Getty: 33cl, 33bl, 34tl.
Mark Leech: 43bl.
PA Photos: Lewis Whyld 44cla.
Popperfoto: 51cl; 60bl; 62cl.

ProZone Sports Ltd: 59cr.
Rex Features: NWI 56bl.
Sporting Pictures (uk) Ltd: 2cr, 22cl, 23tl, 23tr, 36bl.

Wall chart: Colorsport: cl (Arthur Rowe), cla; DK Images: Football Museum, Preston tl (Lord Kinnaird), tl (Chinese characters); Getty Images: © 1974 FIFA™ / David Leah / Mexsport crb; Time & Life Pictures ca (Pele)

Jacket images: *Front:* **Alamy:** Alto Foto c; **DK Images:** Football Museum, Preston tc, tr; **PA Photos:** Peter Robinson tl. *Back:* **DK Images:** Football Museum, Preston bl, br, c, cl, cr, cla, tl, tr.

All other images © Dorling Kindersley
For further information see:
www.dkimages.com